STANISLAVSKI:
AN INTRODUCTION

Books by Stanislavski

An Actor Prepares
An Actor's Handbook
Building A Character
Creating A Role
My Life in Art
Stanislavski's Legacy

By Jean Benedetti

Stanislavski: A Biography
The Moscow Art Theatre Letters

STANISLAVSKI: AN INTRODUCTION

Jean Benedetti

Theatre Arts Books
Routledge, New York

First published in Great Britain in 1982 as a paperback original
by Methuen London Ltd.
Reprinted 1985 and 1986

Revised and reprinted in 1989
by Methuen Drama
an imprint of Reed Consumer Books Ltd
Michelin House, 81 Fulham Road, London SW3 6RB
and Auckland, Melbourne, Singapore and Toronto

Reprinted 1990, 1991 (twice), 1992

Published in North America by
Theatre Arts, Routledge,
29 West 35th Street, New York, NY 10001

ISBN 0-413-50030-6

Printed and bound in Great Britain
by Cox & Wyman Ltd, Reading, Berks.

Contents

List of Abbreviations

Works regularly referred to are indicated by the following abbreviations. All other works are indicated by their title in full.

By Stanislavski

SS   *Sobranie Sochinenii* (Collected Works), 8 vols, Moscow, 1951–1964.

MLIA   *My Life in Art*, Methuen London, 1980.

AAP   *An Actor Prepares*, Methuen London, 1980.

BAC   *Building A Character*, Methuen London, 1979.

CAR   *Creating a Role*, Methuen London, 1981.

SL   *Stanislavski's Legacy*, Methuen London, 1981.

KSA   Stanislavski Archives, MXAT Museum, Moscow.

By others

SD   *Stanislavski Directs*, Nikolai M. Gorchakov, Minerva Press, New York, 1954.

SIR   *Stanislavski in Rehearsal*, Vasily Toporkov, Theatre Arts Books, New York, 1979.

MLIRT   *My Life in the Russian Theatre*, Vladimir Nemirovich-Danchenko, Theatre Arts Books, New York, 1968.

A Brief Chronology

The following biographical events are referred to in the text. Production dates indicate the first night, not the beginning of rehearsals.

1863   Konstantin Sergeyevich Alexeyev (Stanislavski) born.
1877   The Alexeyev Circle formed.
1883   Stanislavski spends brief period at a drama school. Meets Glikeria Fedotova for the first time.
1888   Is directed by Fedotov in *Les Plaideurs* of Racine and Gogol's *The Gambler*.
        Foundation of The Society of Art and Literature.
        Is directed by Fedotov in Molière's *Georges Dandin*.
1890   Second Russian tour of the Meiningen Company.
1896   Plays Othello.
1897   Meeting with Nemirovich-Danchenko. Foundation of the Moscow Art Theatre (MXAT).
1898   MXAT opens (October 14) with Stanislavski's production of Alexei Tolstoy's *Tsar Fyodor Ioannovich*.
        Directs *The Seagull*,* plays Trigorin (December).
1899   Directs *Hedda Gabler*, plays Lövborg (February).
        Directs première of *Uncle Vanya*,* plays Astrov (October).
1900   Directs *An Enemy of the People*, plays Dr Stockmann (October).
1901   Directs première of *Three Sisters*,* plays Vershinin (January).
        Directs *The Wild Duck* (September).
1902   Directs première of Gorki's *Small People* (October) and première of *The Lower Depths*,* plays Satin (December).
1903   Plays Brutus in *Julius Caesar*.
1904   Directs première of *The Cherry Orchard*,* plays Gaev (January).

* Indicates a collaboration with Nemirovich-Danchenko.

1905   Directs *Ghosts** (March) and première of Gorki's *Children of the Sun** (October).

1906   German tour by MXAT.
             Crisis of confidence.
             Summer holiday in Finland. Beginning of the System.

1907   Directs Knut Hamsun's *The Drama of Life* (February) and Andreyev's *The Life of Man* (December).

1909   Directs *A Month in the Country*, plays Rakitin (December).

1910   Plays in Ostrovski's *Enough Stupidity in Every Wise Man* (March).

1911   Craig's *Hamlet* at MXAT (December).

1915   Directs and plays in Pushkin's *Mozart and Salieri* and *The Miser Knight* (March).

1920   Directs Byron's *Cain* (April).

1922–3   American tour.

1924   American edition of *My Life in Art*.

1926   Russian edition (revised) of *My Life in Art*.

1930   Writes production plan for *Othello*.

1936   American edition of *An Actor Prepares*, second Russian edition (revised) of *My Life in Art*.

1938   Rehearses *Tartuffe*. Dies before opening.
             Russian edition of *An Actor Prepares*.

Introduction

The Stanislavski Stystem is not an abstraction; it is an activity and a practice. It is a working method for working actors. It is a system because it is coherent, logical – systematic. Anyone who imagines that the System will yield results through a purely intellectual, detached comprehension of its basic ideas will be disappointed. The System is not a theoretical construct; it is a *process*. The texts of Stanislavski which we possess are a guide to that process and an invitation to experience it directly, personally and creatively.

The texts, however, are more complicated than they at first seem. Stanislavski only saw two books through the press, *My Life in Art* (first published in America, 1924) and *An Actor Prepares* (first published in America, 1936). The other texts which we possess, *Building A Character* and *Creating a Role* are editorial reconstructions based on existing drafts and notes. All the books, moreover, with the possible exception of *My Life in Art*, which was revised twice, in 1926 and 1936, were regarded by Stanislavski as provisional. The Archives contain revisions and new material which were intended for subsequent editions.

The aim of the present book is to provide a framework in which the available texts can be read, to supply supplementary information which will make their meaning clearer and to place them in the context of the sequence of books which Stanislavski planned but did not live to complete.

It is in no sense a biography. In so far as the System results from Stanislavski's analysis of his own career, biographical elements are used to demonstrate the origin and evolution of his ideas. A complete personal portrait, however, is not attempted. Where necessary, lines of enquiry are pursued out of chronological sequence. When certain basic positions to which Stanislavski adhered all his life are under discussion, readers, will, therefore, find quotations drawn from different periods.

Wherever possible quotations are taken from English-language editions. There are, however, substantial differences between the English texts and the eight-volume Soviet edition of the Complete

Works. Where a choice has been necessary, the Soviet edition has been preferred. An outline of the major differences is given in the Appendix. I am greatly indebted to the scholarly introductions to the individual volumes of the Complete Works by G. Kristi and V. H. Prokoviev. I have also been greatly helped by two seminars on the Stanislavski System arranged by the Soviet Centre of the International Theatre Institute in October 1979 and April 1981 when it was possible to consult leading Soviet directors, actors and teachers on the later developments and workings of Stanislavski's methods. I would, in addition, like to thank Professor Alexei Bartoshevich, professor of Theatre History at GITIS (State Institute for Theatre Arts) for his generous advice and guidance. Any misunderstandings are, of course, entirely my own.

J.B.

Introduction to the Second Edition

In the seven years since this book was written much new material on Stanislavski's life and work has been published in the Soviet Union and more new material is promised in the forthcoming nine-volume *Complete Works*. Some of this information has been made available in discussion. My recent researches in preparing a new biography of Stanislavski have caused me to modify my interpretation of certain aspects of his work and personality. Thus, while the main argument of the book remains constant, it does seem appropriate to provide significant new facts and to modify certain points of emphasis.

J.B., October, 1988

1

Foundations

Had Stanislavski been a 'natural', had his talent – some would say his genius – as an actor found an immediate, spontaneous outlet, there would be no System. As it was it took years of persistent, unremitting effort to remove the blocks and barriers which inhibited the free expression of his great gifts. His search for the 'laws' of acting was the result of that struggle.

Stanislavski's career might be described as the painful evolution of a stage-struck child into a mature and responsible artist and teacher. He remained stage-struck to the end, adoring the smell of spirit-gum and grease-paint. His infatuation with theatre, with play-acting kept his mind fresh and open to new ideas to the very end. At the same time theatre was, for him, a matter of the highest seriousness, both artistic and moral. It was a disciplined activity which required dedication and training. What we receive as the System originated from his attempt to analyse and monitor his own progress as an artist and his attempts to achieve his ideals as an actor and meet his own developing standards, and it is all the more valuable for being born of concrete activity since the solutions he found were lived and not the result of speculation or abstract theory. The System is his practice examined, tested and verified. Although he received help along the way from actors and directors the System is essentially Stanislavski's own creation. For, while others could define for him the results that were required, they could not define the process by which those results might be achieved. This he had to do for himself. *My Life in Art* is the story (not always accurate) of his failures, false starts and successes.

Stanislavski was born in 1863, the second son of a family devoted to the theatre. He made his first stage appearance at the age of seven in a series of tableaux vivants organised by his governess to celebrate his mother's name day. When he was fourteen his father transformed an out-building on his country estate at Liubimovka into a well-equipped theatre.[1] Later, a second theatre was constructed in the town house in Moscow. Stanislavski's real début as an actor was made

[1] MLIA Chap. VI.

at Liubimovka in September 1877, when four one-act plays, directed
by his tutor, were staged to inaugurate the new theatre. As a result of
that evening an amateur group, the Alexeyev Circle[1], was formed,
consisting of Stanislavski's brothers and sisters, cousins and one or
two friends.

It is at this date that Stanislavski's conscious, artistic career can
be said to begin. During the period 1877 to 1906, which he describes
as his Childhood and Adolescence,[2] he encountered the fundamental problems of acting and directing which he resolved as best
he could.

He spent the day of that 5 September, according to his own
account[3], in a state of extreme excitement, trembling all over in
his eagerness to get on stage. In the event the performance was
to produce more perplexity than satisfaction. He appeared in two
of the plays, *A Cup of Tea* and *The Old Mathematician*. In the
first he felt completely at ease. He was able to copy the performance
of a famous actor he had seen, down to the last detail. When the
curtain fell he was convinced he had given a splendid performance. He was soon disabused. He had been inaudible. He had
gabbled and his hands had been in such a constant state of motion that
no one could follow what he was saying. In the second play, which had
given him so much more trouble in rehearsals, he was, by contrast,
much better. He was at a loss to resolve the contradiction between
what he felt and what the audience had experienced. How could he
feel so good and act so badly? Feel so ill at ease and be so effective?

His response to the problem was crucial. He began to keep a
notebook, in which he recorded his impressions, analysed his difficulties and sketched out solutions. He continued this practice
throughout his life, so that the Notebooks span some sixty-one years
of activity.[4] It is characteristic of Stanislavski that he never shied
away from contradictions or refused the paradoxical. He worked
through them.

His frequent visits to the theatre provided him with models and
examples. At the Maly Theatre – his 'university' – as he called
it – there were still the survivors of a once great company. He
was also able to see foreign artists such as Salvini and Duse, who

[1] Alexeyev was the family name. Stanislavski was a stage name.
[2] MLIA Chaps I–XLVII.
[3] MLIA pp. 62–3.
[4] Extracts from the Notebooks are printed in Cole and Chinoy (eds.),
Actors on Acting, pp. 485–90.

appeared in Moscow during Lent, when Russian actors were for-
bidden by the church to perform. The contrast between the ease,
naturalness and flow of the actor of genius and his own desperate
efforts, either gabbling inaudibly or shouting, either rigid with tension or all flailing arms, made a profound effect on him. They
created, he could only imitate more or less well what others had
done before.[1] The attempt to discover in what the 'naturalness' of the
great actor consisted is the seed from which the System grew.

Drama school

In 1885, at the age of twenty-two Stanislavski entered a drama
school. The experience lasted three weeks. His rapid departure was
caused partly by the fact that he could not attend full-time. He had
finished his studies early and gone into the family textile business.
He could not always get away from the office. More imporant, however, was his swift recognition of the fact that the school could not
give him what he was looking for – a properly thought-out method of
working, a means of harnessing his own natural creativity. Not only
did the school fail to provide such a method, it could not even con-
ceive that such a method existed. All his teachers could do was
indicate the results they wanted, not the means to achieve them.
At best, they could pass on the technical tricks which they themselves had acquired.[2]

   The young Stanislavski needed guidance and discipline badly.
The greater barrier to his development as an artist was his image
of himself as an actor. He saw himself continuously in dashing
'romantic' roles. It was what he himself defined as his 'Spanish
boots' problem. Thigh boots, a sword and a cloak were fatal to
him. Any progress he might have made towards truth and naturalness was immediately wiped out. He became a musical–comedy
stereotype – all swagger and bombast. The only teacher at drama
school who might have been some help to him, Glikeria Fedotova,
left about the same time he did. He was fortunate enough to meet
her again later, as well as her husband, at a critical moment in
his career.

[1] MLIA p. 74.
[2] MLIA pp. 85–8.

A theatre in decline

Russian theatre in the last quarter of the nineteenth century was in a poor state. There were the great stars of the Maly Theatre whom Stanislavski describes in terms of such admiration and affection,[1] but they were mainly of the older generation and they were surrounded by mediocrity. The monopoly of the imperial theatres had been abolished in 1882. Thereafter commercial managements threw on plays to make quick profits. As Stanislavski remarked, the theatre was controlled by barmen on one hand and bureaucrats on the other. A few brilliant individuals shone here and there.[2]

On the whole observation of professional practice could only show Stanislavski what to avoid. In an unpublished manuscript he describes a typical rehearsal period. First came the reading and the casting of the various roles. Some discussion of the play's meaning was supposed to take place but generally there was insufficient time. The actors were left to find their own way. Then came the first rehearsal.

> It took place on stage with a few old tables and chairs as a set. The director explained the decor: a door centre, two doors on each side etc.
>
> At the first rehearsal the actors read their parts book in hand and the prompter was silent. The director sat on the forestage and gave his instructions to the cast. 'What should I do here?' asked one actor. 'Sit on the sofa,' the director answers. 'And what should I be doing?' asks another. 'You are nervous, wring your hands and walk up and down,' the director orders. 'Can't I sit down?' the actor persists. 'How can you possibly sit down when you are nervous?' replies the bewildered director. So the first and second acts are set. On the next day, that is to say the second rehearsal, work continues in like manner with the third and fourth acts. The third and sometimes the fourth rehearsal consist of going through the whole thing again; the actors move about the stage, memorizing the director's instructions, reading their lines in half-voice i.e. a whisper, gesticulating strongly in an attempt to arouse some feeling.
>
> At the next rehearsal the lines must be known. In theatres

[1] MLIA Chap. IX.
[2] SS Vol. 1, p. 181.

with money this may last one or two days, and another rehearsal is arranged where the actors play without script but still at half voice. The prompter, however, works at full voice.

At the next rehearsal the actors are expected to play at full voice. Then dress rehearsals begin with make-up, costumes and the set. Finally there is the performance.[1]

This seems to have been a comparatively disciplined affair. More often than not the actors simply took over, ignoring the director, settling for what they knew best. An actress would move to the window or the fireplace for no better reason than that was what she always did.[2] The script meant less than nothing. Sometimes the cast did not even bother to learn their lines. Leading actors would simply plant themselves downstage centre, by the prompter's box, wait to be fed the lines and then deliver them straight at the audience in a ringing voice, giving a fine display of passion and 'temperament'. Everyone, in fact, spoke their lines out front. Direct communication with other actors was minimal. Furniture was so arranged as to allow the actors to face front.

Sets were as stereotyped as the acting: wings, back-drops taken from stock, doors conventionally placed, standing isolated in space with no surrounding wall. The costumes were also 'typical'. When Stanislavski attempted to have costumes made to specific designs he was told, with some asperity, that there were standard designs for character types and would continue to be.[3] There was no sense of a need for change or renewal. The amateur theatre reflected the practice of the professional, only worse.[4]

If Stanislavski wanted models or guidance he would have to look back a generation or so earlier, to the great days of the Maly Theatre when artistic standards had been set and discipline imposed by two men of genius, the actor Mikhail Shchepkin and the writer Nikolai Gogol. The actors Stanislavski so admired were impressive not merely because they had talent but because they had been trained in this school, where the first steps had been taken towards a genuinely Russian theatre and the creation of a genuinely Russian style – Realism.

[1] KSA no. 1353 pp. 1–7. The prompter here speaks the text continuously, as in opera. The box is placed downstage centre on a level with the footlights.
[2] MLIRT pp. 96–8.
[3] MLIA Chap. XVI.
[4] MLIA Chap. XIV.

Shchepkin

Mikhail Shchepkin (1788–1863) was born a serf on the estate of
Count Wolkenstein. It was common practice among members of
the Russian aristocracy in the eighteenth century to create companies of actors composed of their more talented serfs. These serfs
not infrequently received an education at the same level as the
children of their masters.

The prevailing acting style was even more conventionalised than
during Stanislavski's youth. Actors sang their lines in a high declamatory tone. According to Shchepkin's *Memoirs*

> The actors' playing was considered good when none of them
> spoke in his natural voice, but in a totally artificial tone, when
> the words were delivered in a loud voice and when each of them
> was accompanied by a gesture. The words 'love', 'passion',
> 'treachery' were shouted as loudly as possible but the facial ex-
> pression did not add to the effect since it remained invariably
> tense and unnatural.[1]

On making an exit it was obligatory to raise the right hand. Moreover, it was considered impolite for an actor to turn his back on
the audience so that all exits had to be made facing front. Members
of the cast spent a great deal of time, effort and ingenuity in de-
vising methods of getting off stage without infringing this rule.

Conventions of staging were equally rigid. The acting area was
divided into two parts, upstage to downstage, one mobile, the other
immobile. The immobile area, where the actors posed impressively,
was reserved for the aristocratic characters, whose house was represented on that side of the stage. The mobile area was the province
of characters coming from the outside world, the lower orders,
whose manner of delivery was more agitated, i.e. less dignified.
Alternatively, the stage could be divided horizontally, from left to
right; principal roles downstage, supporting roles centre stage,
minor roles upstage.

These were the conventions in which Shchepkin, who displayed
talent early, was educated. In 1810, however, he saw Prince Mish-
cherski in a comedy by Soumarov, *The Supposed Dowry*. The
prince's acting style was quite different from the rest of the cast.
There was an almost total absence of gestures and his delivery was

[1] Shchepkin, Mikhail, *Zhizn i Tvorchestvo* Vol. 1, p. 104 (Moscow 1984).

natural. Shchepkin records in his *Memoirs* that he was not, at first, impressed. This was not 'acting'. This was too much like real life. And yet, there were impressive moments.

> It is curious, but despite the simplicity of his playing, which I considered an inability to act properly, when, as his part progressed, there was any question of money you could see how his soul was wracked and, at that moment, we forgot all the other actors. The fear of death, the fear of losing his money were striking and horrifying in the prince's playing and were by no means diminished by the simple style in which he spoke.[1]

By the end of the performance Shchepkin was asking himself whether the prince was not right and he, wrong.

Some time later he found himself playing the same role and not succeeding. He could not speak naturally on the stage; his declamatory habits were too ingrained. It was no good trying to imitate the prince if he could not create the internal process by which Meshcherski had achieved his results.

An accident came to the rescue. One day he was rehearsing Sganarelle in Molière's *School for Husbands*. He was tired and running out of energy and began 'just saying' the lines. The result was a revelation.

> I realised that I had said a few words in a perfectly simple manner, so simple that had I said them in life and not in a play I would not have said them otherwise.[2]

The way was open to a new style of acting – Realism. It was the genius of Shchepkin to have taken what he initially, in common with his fellow actors, considered incompetence and turned it into a new and positive method of work.

Shchepkin's reputation grew. His admirers planned to buy his freedom and, after some difficulties, succeeded in 1822. The following year he joined the Imperial Theatre in Moscow and in 1824 appeared in the opening performance, on 14 October, of the Maly Theatre.[3]

He played continuously at the Maly for forty years, so that the theatre, in time, came to be known as the House of Shchepkin,

[1] Shchepkin, op. cit. pp. 102–3.
[2] Ibid. p. 104.
[3] Maly (Little) as opposed to Bolshoi (Big) where opera and ballet were presented.

much as the Comédie Française is known as La Maison de Molière. Pushkin, Gogol, Lermontov and Griboyedov were among his admirers.

Shchepkin insisted that it was the actor's job to 'crawl under the skin' of the character, identify with his thoughts and feelings so as to produce a living portrait.[1] The actor's material was drawn from knowledge in himself and, above all, observation of life. Such a task required application and discipline.

> It is so much easier to play mechanically – for that you only need your reason. Reason will approach sorrow and joy to the same extent that any imitation can approach nature. But an actor of feeling – that's something else again. Indescribable labours await him. He must begin by wiping out his self . . . and become the character the author intended him to be. He must walk, talk, think, feel, cry, laugh – as the author wants him to. You see how the work of the actor is more meaningful. In the first case you need only pretend to live – in the second you have to live. . . . You might say that this is impossible. No, it is only difficult. You may say, why struggle with some kind of perfection when there are much simpler means of pleasing the audience? One can only answer to that, why have art?[2]

Shchepkin imposed strict discipline on himself. In a career spanning fifty years he never missed a rehearsal and was never late. He expected no less dedication from others.

> We have not yet achieved a proper idea of real application to work, so we must watch ourselves otherwise we shall fall into the typical Russian attitude of perhaps and maybe, which, in art, produces nothing.[3]

For Shchepkin the actor's individuality, his own particular way of doing and saying things, was of paramount importance. At the same time all the actor's gifts and talents had to be subordinated to the central theme of the play.

---

[1] Letter to Alexandra Schubert: Cole and Chinoy (eds.), *Actors on Acting*, New York, Crown, 1970, p. 483.
[2] Ibid.
[3] Shchepkin, op. cit. pp. 278–9.

Gogol

He found a natural ally in Gogol (1809–52). Indeed such was the identity of their views that it is a matter of scholarly dispute as to who influenced whom the most. Gogol himself was an extremely gifted actor. Significantly he failed an audition for the Imperial Theatre because his performance was too simple, too 'real'.

Actor and author made common cause against the current repertoire which consisted mainly of imitations of French theatre. They succeeded through their work at the Maly in creating a theatre which had something to say about contemporary Russian society and an acting style which was based on truthful observation and not convention.

Gogol expressed his ideas in the *Petersburg Notes of 1836*, his *Advice to Those Who Would Play 'The Government Inspector' as It Ought to be Played* (*c.* 1846) and in his letters.

Of the contemporary repertoire he said:

> The strange has become the subject of contemporary drama ... murders, fires, the wildest passions which have no place in contemporary society! ... Hangmen, poisons – a constant straining for effect; not a single character inspires any sympathy whatsoever! No spectator ever leaves the theatre touched, in tears; on the contrary, he clambers into his carriage hurriedly, in an anxious state and is unable to collect his thoughts for a long time.[1]

Of the effect on the actor:

> The situation of the Russian actor is pitiful. All about him a young nation pulsates and seethes and they give him characters he has never set eyes upon. What can he do with these strange heroes, who are neither Frenchmen nor Germans but bizarre people totally devoid of definite passions and distinct features? Where can he display his art? On what can he develop his talent? For heaven's sake give us Russian characters, give us ourselves – our scoundrels, our eccentrics.... Truly it is high time we learned that only a faithful rendering of characters – not in general stereotyped features but in national forms so striking in their vitality that we are compelled to exclaim: 'Yes, that

[1] *The Theater of Nikolay Gogol*, pp. 166–7.

person seems familiar to me' – only such a rendering can be of genuine service. . . .

We have turned the theatre into a plaything . . . something like a rattle used to entice children, forgetting that it is a rostrum from which a living lesson is spoken to an entire multitude. . . .[1]

More specifically he advised actors:

Above all beware of falling into caricature. Nothing ought to be exaggerated or hackneyed, not even the minor roles. . . . The less an actor thinks about being funny or making the audience laugh, the more the comic elements of his part will come through. The ridiculous will emerge spontaneously through the very seriousness with which each character is occupied with his own affairs. They are all caught up in their own interests, bustling and fussing, even fervent, as if faced with the most important task of their lives. Only the audience, from its detached position, can perceive the vanity of their concerns. But they themselves do not joke at all, and have no inkling that anybody is laughing at them. The intelligent actor, before seizing upon the petty oddities and superficial peculiarities of his part, must strive to capture those aspects that are *common to all mankind*. He ought to consider the purpose of his role, the major and predominant concern of each character, what it is that consumes his life and constitutes the perpetual object of his thoughts, his *idée fixe*. Having grasped this major concern, the actor must assimilate it so thoroughly that the thoughts and yearnings of his character seem to be his own and remain constantly in his mind over the course of the performance. . . . So, one should first grasp the soul of a part not its dress.[2]

Writing to Shchepkin on 16 December 1846, he said:

It is essential that you replay each role, if only in your mind; that you feel the unity of the play and read it through to the actors several times, so that they might involuntarily assimilate the true meaning of every phrase. . . , introduce . . . the actors to the proper essence of their roles, to a dignified and correct measure in their speech – do you understand? – a false note must not be heard. . . . Root out caricature entirely and lead them to understand that an actor must not *present* but *transmit*.

[1] Ibid.
[2] *Nikolay Gogol*, pp. 169–70.

He must, first of all, transmit ideas, forgetting about a person's oddities and peculiarities.[1]

Stanislavski came to regard himself as the natural successor to Shchepkin. Symbolically, perhaps, he was born on the day Shchepkin died, 18 January 1863.

Realism

Stanislavski does not provide any ordered account of the manner in which he became familiar with Shchepkin's teachings. Shchepkin is there in *My Life in Art* as an all-pervading presence. On pages 85–6 there is a substantial quotation from a letter to the actor Shumsky which Stanislavski describes as being of 'tremendous, practical importance'. In the Stanislavski Archives a copiously annotated edition of Shchepkin's *Letters* is to be found. In 1908, on the tenth anniversary of the Moscow Art Theatre, Stanislavski publicly reaffirmed his intention of continuing in the path laid down by Shchepkin. In so doing he placed himself firmly side by side with Gogol, Ostrovski and the Realist tradition.

Stanislavski's mature activity can only be understood if it is seen as rooted in the conviction that the theatre is a moral instrument whose function is to civilise, to increase sensitivity, to heighten perception and, in terms perhaps now unfashionable to us, to ennoble the mind and uplift the spirit. The best method of achieving this end was adherence to the principles of Realism. This was more than a question of aesthetic preference or a predilection for one 'style' over other 'styles'. It was a question of asserting the primacy of the human content of theatre over other considerations, of content over form. Stanislavski was implaccably opposed to meaningless conventions, to 'Theatre' in the theatre, which he hated. He was no less opposed, later in life, to the experiments of the avant-garde, which he considered reduced the actor to a mechanical object. Dehumanised actors lead to dehumanised perceptions.

It is important to define what Stanislavski understood by the term Realism and to distinguish it from Naturalism, a word which he normally employed in a purely pejorative sense. Naturalism, for him, implied the indiscriminate reproduction of the surface of life. Realism, on the other hand, while taking its material from the real world and from direct observation, selected only those elements which revealed the relationships and tendencies lying

[1] Op. cit., p. 177.

under the surface. The rest was discarded. Speaking to the cast of *Woe from Wit* in 1924, in terms which closely echo Gogol, Stanislavski said:

> We have often been and still are accused of falling into a Naturalistic expression of detail in our pursuit of the Realism of life and truth in our stage actions. Wherever we have done this we were wrong.... Realism in art is the method which helps to select only the typical from life. If at times we are Naturalistic in our stage work, it only shows that we don't yet know enough to be able to penetrate into the historical and social essence of events and characters. We do not know how to separate the main from the secondary, and thus we bury the idea with details of the mode of life. That is my understanding of Naturalism.[1]

Speaking to Nikolai M. Gorchakov, then a young director in 1926, he said:

> I want you to remember this fundamental theatrical rule: establish truly and precisely details that are typical and the audience will have a sense of the whole, because of their special ability to imagine and complete in imagination what you have suggested.
>
> But the detail must be characteristic and typical of whatever you want the audience to see. That is why Naturalism is poisonous to the theatre. Naturalism cheats the audience of its main pleasure and its most important satisfaction, that of creating with the actor and completing in its imagination what the actor, the director and the designer suggest with their techniques.[2]

In insisting on the social function of the theatre Stanislavski placed himself within a tradition that went back far beyond Gogol. Peter the Great created theatres expressly to further his campaign for the westernisation of his kingdom. His successor, Catherine the Great, went one step further, writing plays, which were performed, anonymously, with the overt intention of educating her people.

The theatre is the school of the people and must be under my

[1] SD p. 143.
[2] SD p. 333.

control. I am the head teacher and must answer to God for my
people's conduct.[1]

Towards the end of his life Stanislavski told a story to Vasily
Toporkov, which illustrates the strength of his conviction. He was
on tour in Petersburg. Rehearsals had gone on into the early hours
of the morning. Coming out of the theatre he saw a crowd of
people. It was a frosty night and bonfires had been lit in the
square:

> Some were warming themselves at the bonfires, rubbing their
> hands, legs, ears; others were standing in groups, arguing
> spiritedly. Smoke from the bonfires arose, the crowd murmured
> in a thousand voices. What was this? 'These people are waiting
> for tickets for your production,' I thought. 'My God, what a
> responsibility we have to satisfy the spiritual needs of these
> people who have been standing here freezing all night; what great
> ideas and thoughts we must bring to them.'
> So, consider well, whether we have the right to settle accounts
> with them by merely telling them a funny anecdote.... I felt
> that the people whom I had seen in the square deserved much
> more than we had prepared for them.[2]

Stanislavski remained, however, consistently opposed to 'political'
theatre. If the theatre was in Gogol's words a 'pulpit from which
it is one's duty to educate the audience', the actor was not to
preach directly. It was not his function to tell the spectator what
to think. The message of the play must be implicit; it must become apparent through the careful process of selection which takes
place during rehearsals and the truthful presentation of the material
agreed upon. It was not enough to persuade the intellect or convince
the intelligence; the theatre had to give a total human experience
which the audience could feel with its whole being. This experience
would have longer, deeper resonances than the mere acknowledge-
ment of the truth of a concept. Stanislavski's experience both before and after the Revolution convinced him of this. In 1901 he
was playing Dr Stockman in Ibsen's *An Enemy of the People* in
Petersburg. On 4 March a demonstration took place on Kazan
Square. A number of people were killed. When Stanislavski, in
Act Five delivered the line, 'You should never put on a new pair

[1] Evreinov, op. cit., p. 172.
[2] SIR pp. 200–1.

of trousers when you go out to fight for freedom and truth', the audience erupted.

> Spontaneously the audience connected the line with the massacre in Kazan Square, where, without a doubt many a new suit had been ripped apart in the name of liberty and truth. These words provoked such a storm of applause that we had to stop the performance. The audience stood up and rushed towards the footlights, holding out their arms to me. That day I learned, through my own personal experience, the great power which real, authentic theatre can have on people.[1]

And yet in Stanislavski's mind and in the mind of the rest of the cast there was no conscious connection between the events of the play and the current political situation.

> Perhaps in choosing this particular play and interpreting the roles in that particular way we were responding intuitively to the prevailing state of mind in society and the conditions of life in our country where people were waiting passionately for a hero who would fearlessly proclaim the truth which the government and censorship suppressed. But, when we were on stage we interpreted the play with no thought of politics.... As for the 'message' of the play, I did not discover it, it revealed itself to me.[2]

He concludes with a question:

> For a social and political play to have an effect on the audience, isn't the secret for the actor to think as little as possible of the social and political intentions of the play so as to be perfectly sincere and perfectly honest?[3]

When, four years later, he came to direct Gorki's *The Lower Depths* he adopted the opposite approach. The result was, in his view a failure. He was too aware of the political and social importance of the play and nothing got over the footlights. Thus he concluded that the actor's task was to present a fully rounded character; it was the audience's job to find the political meaning.[4] This they would derive from the total production. As he matured and developed Stanislavski became convinced of the need for an ideo-

[1] SS Vol. 1, p. 250.
[2] Ibid.
[3] SS Vol. 1, p. 251.
[4] MLIA pp. 406–7.

logical analysis of the script and for an awareness of the audience for which the performance was intended but, in production terms, this analysis had to express itself in terms of concrete action – moves, gestures, words – not overt comment.[1] The meaning of the events presented on stage must be *transparent*. The audience must be able to see and understand the behaviour of the characters, the reasons for their actions and decisions and at the same time participate in the process, living the action with them.[2]

A theatre, conceived not as a histrionic showcase but as a place in which to promote understanding, demanded that the actor see himself and his particular creative contribution as part of an *ensemble*. In 1890 Stanislavski saw the Meiningen company from Germany on their second tour of Russia. Unaccountably he had missed their first tour in 1885. There he saw what a disciplined company could achieve. The actors, on the whole, were mediocre. Ostrovski, writing of the first tour, was highly critical. Stanislavski, none the less, was struck by the coherence of the performance of *Julius Caesar* which he saw and in particular by the effectiveness of the crowd scenes. Much of the success was due to the iron hand with which the director, Chronegk[3], ruled his actors. The performance was created out of the will and conception of the director, not out of the creative energy of the actors. It was a tempting but highly dangerous example. It was, however, one of the few examples available.

If much was to be expected of actors in terms of application, dedication and discipline, Stanislavski realised, it was important that they should be treated with respect and given decent conditions to work in. In his first incursions into the professional theatre he was appalled at the filthy state of the theatre and the primitive nature of the dressing rooms. It was a situation which he quickly put to rights.

The Moscow Art Theatre (*MXAT*)

Stanislavski came to intellectual and artistic maturity in the fourteen years between 1883, when he was twenty-three and 1897, when he was thirty-four. This was in no small measure due to the work

---

[1] SD pp. 134–8.
[2] SD p. 45.
[3] Spelled 'Kronek' in MLIA.

he accomplished with the Society of Art and Literature, which he founded with a group of friends in 1888.[1] The ideas which he developed during that period were finally enshrined in the policy of the Moscow Art Theatre (MXAT).

In June 1897 Stanislavski received two letters from Vladimir Nemirovich-Danchenko suggesting a meeeting. He replied by telegram: 'Will be glad to meet you June 21 at 2 o'clock at Slavyanski Bazaar.[2] The discussion lasted eighteen hours ending at Stanislavski's villa at eight the next morning, by which time the policy of MXAT had broadly been worked out.

Nemirovich-Danchenko (1858–1943) was a successful playwright. In 1896 he had won the Griboyedov prize for *The Worth of Life* although he protested that the award should have gone to Chekhov's *Seagull*, which had just received its disastrous première at the Alexandrinsky Theatre in Petersburg. Nemirovich's plays were regularly presented at the Maly. In 1890 he had been asked to take over the acting classes at the Philharmonic school. Among his pupils were Olga Knipper, later to be Chekhov's wife, Meyerhold and Ivan Moskvin. Nemirovich shared Stanislavski's dissatisfaction with the state of Russian theatre. The two men had reached identical conclusions on the reforms that were necessary. It was logical that they should meet. Yet, initially, Nemirovich had reservations. Stanislavski was rich, he seemed to play anything and everything, and also direct. What if he were no more than a wealthy dilettante, whose sole desire was to hog all the leading roles? Nemirovich was reassured however by the fact that Fedotova, who by then had worked with Stanislavski and whose judgement he trusted, referred affectionately to him as her 'Kostya'.

Nemirovich has left a much more detailed account of the eighteen-hour meeting than Stanislavski himself.[3] In it he describes not only the decisions they took but the abuses against which they were reacting. Stanislavski himself later compared the scope of their discussions to the Treaty of Versailles.[4] Nemirovich speaks of his pleasure in discovering that they shared a common working method – detailed discussions and reading followed by slow meticulous rehearsal, section by section.

MXAT was more than the culmination of two men's aspirations;

[1] See Chapter Two.
[2] MLIRT p. 75.
[3] MLIRT pp. 79–113.
[4] MLIA p. 294.

it was the embodiment of the reforms which Pushkin, Gogol, Ostrovski and Shchepkin had advocated over three-quarters of a century. It brought to fruition the dreams and ideals of the past and broke, finally, with the tired routine and the outworn clichés which stifled any creative impulse.

The first concern was to create a genuine ensemble, with no star players – 'Today Hamlet, tomorrow an extra'. Self-centred, false, histrionic actors were rigorously excluded.[1] All productions were to be created from scratch, with their own sets and costumes. Working conditions were to be decent and comfortable. Discipline was to be strict, both for the cast – no talking in the corridors during a performance – and for the audience. No one was to be allowed back-stage during the performance and spectators were to be encouraged to take their seats before the curtain went up. With the passage of time late-comers were made to wait until the interval before being admitted. The orchestra, which was a regular feature in most theatres, was abolished as an unnecessary distraction.

When the original theatre was built, the auditorium was stripped of all decoration so that the audience's full concentration could be directed towards the stage. Everything, including the administration, was subordinated to the process of creation. Nemirovich had too many unpleasant memories of the bureaucracy of the imperial theatres.

It was agreed that responsibility for artistic policy should be divided between the two men. Stanislavski was to have the last word in all matters concerning the production, Nemirovich in all matters concerning repertoire and scripts. As Nemirovich put it, they divided form and content between them.

Finally there was the question of the kind of public they wanted to attract. Neither of them had much time for the fashionable Moscow audiences. Both wanted a popular theatre which would fulfil its mission to enlighten and educate the people. Originally they planned to call their new theatre The Moscow Art Theatre Open to All. They hoped by not using the word 'popular' to avoid problems with the censor. But their dreams of presenting free performances to working-class audiences soon came to grief. There was a special censor for all plays presented to workers. This would have meant clearing scripts with no fewer than four separate

[1] MLIA pp. 294–5.

censors. Nemirovich was in fact warned that if he persisted in his idea of presenting special workers' performances he would be liable to arrest. The scheme was abandoned and the name shortened simply to the Moscow Art Theatre.[1]

The importance of the new theatre's policy lay not in the originality of any of its elements, but in its organic unity. The Meiningen company had shown what ensemble playing could achieve. On his trips to France on behalf of the family business Stanislavski had seen the work of Antoine and his Théâtre Libre. Strindberg had published his views on intimate theatre. Carefully researched sets and costumes were not unknown in western Europe. The achievement of MXAT was to bring them all together, consciously and deliberately, and, ultimately to create a style of acting in which the dominant element was human truth.

[1] MLIRT pp. 181–2.

2

The Growth of the System

By the time he came to found MXAT Stanislavski had turned himself into the outstanding actor and director of his time. His own account of his early career in *My Life in Art* must be read with caution. More than an autobiography, it is a justification of the System. His achievements prior to the birth of the System in 1906 are therefore played down, and it is difficult to gain any proper sense of the very great eminence he had achieved by the end of the century. On more than one occasion he had been invited to join the Maly and refused, but nonetheless made guest appearances with the most distinguished members of the company. Many of his contemporaries saw in him the one man with the talent and vision to carry forward the great tradition of Shchepkin, Gogol and Pushkin and revitalise Russian theatre.

He had worked hard during the fourteen years which separated his short period at drama school and his historic meeting with Nemirovich. In his account of this first encounter Nemirovich describes him as giving an impression of graceful and careless ease.[1] There was, moreover, nothing of the 'actor' about him, neither the overpitched voice nor the extravagance of manner. He behaved like a normal human being.

This relaxation had been achieved with difficulty. Stanislavski was very tall and, in his youth, awkward and ungainly. He created an external technique for himself by continuously analysing his own faults, locating his problems – physical tension, lack of vocal stamina, general lack of control over his actions – and working on them. The vocal exercises, the hours spent in front of a mirror are described almost painfully in *My Life in Art*.

There were, however, more fundamental problems concerning his general approach to the art of acting over which he did receive assistance from others: first his lack of method, *any* method, in his playing of a role; second his susceptibility to theatrical cliché as soon as he started to rehearse. Whatever his intellectual percep-

[1] MLIRT pp. 80–81.

tion of the necessity for realism, for truth, for honesty, for observation, time and time again he would fall back on standard formulae. He was greatly helped, however, in tackling these problems by Glikeria Fedotova, whom he had briefly encountered at drama school, and by her husband, a distinguished actor and director.

It was from Fedotova that Stanislavski learned something first-hand of Shchepkin. She had been one of Shchepkin's pupils and Stanislavski recounts some of her experiences in *My Life in Art*.[1] He met her again in 1888 when he took part in a charity performance together with a number of actors from the Maly. This was his first encounter with professionals and he found it disconcerting. He could not match their energy, preparation and discipline. He felt out of his depth. He confided his difficulties to Fedotova and she replied, not unkindly however, that, as an actor, he was a mess. She suggested that working more frequently with her and her colleagues would help him learn.[2]

He was fortunate to meet her again later the same year. Her husband, Fedotov, had recently returned from Paris, where he had been active for some years, and was now anxious to reestablish himself with the Russian public. He decided to direct two plays, *Les Plaideurs* of Racine, in his own translation, and *Gamblers* by Gogol. A number of amateur actors, including Stanislavski, were invited to participate. The experience was decisive. Stanislavski felt he could no longer go on working with amateur groups.[3] Fedotov took him in hand, demonstrated the elements of his role to him, forced him into closer contact with reality.[4]

Out of this chance coming together of a group of actors and artists came the Society of Art and Literature. The company wanted to stay together. Stanislavski himself was at a loose end. The family group, the Alexeyev Circle, had come to a natural end. Marriage, children and family responsibilities left little time for amateur theatricals. Stanislavski's experience with other amateur groups had been disastrous.[5] By a fortunate coincidence the family business had a particularly good year and Stanislavski received an extra

[1] MLIA pp. 80–83.
[2] MLIA pp. 136–7.
[3] MLIA p. 148.
[4] MLIA Chap. XV.
[5] MLIA Chap. XIV.

25–30,000 roubles. This he used to acquire and redecorate premises for the Society.

During the ten years of the Society's existence, Stanislavski was faced with a repertoire of much greater substance than he had encountered hitherto – Pushkin, Molière, Ostrovski, Shakespeare. Up till then his experience had mainly been in lighter forms. He had been successively fascinated by the circus, French farce, operetta, vaudeville and ballet. The new material revealed his lack of method and technique all the more clearly.

Fedotov's production of *Georges Dandin* for the Society in 1888 was of crucial importance to his artistic development. He had seen many productions of Molière in Paris. He arrived, true to form, at rehearsal with every known cliché, every available stereotype, the whole 'orchestration' as Fedotov put it. He was laughed to scorn. Fedotov would have none of it. He took the young actor apart. Stanislavski himself describes it as a surgical operation as the older man cut away all the nonsense. The fact that he was ultimately able to give a good performance was due to the fact that Fedotov demonstrated every move, every gesture. Stanislavski had a model which was not only accomplished in form but original and truthful in conception.[1] But he could not understand the process by which the performance had come into being, nor could Fedotov explain it to him. No one, indeed, seemed capable of explaining it to him.

What Stanislavski did receive from his director was a practical demonstration of what Gogol meant by aiming for essentials, of keeping the meaning of the play perpetually in mind, of building characters round the ideas. Fedotov

> played the plot of the play, but the plot was thoroughly connected with the psychology and the psychology with the image and the poet.[2]

The far-reaching effects of this experience are evident from a letter which he wrote to the French critic Lucien Besnard, some nine years later, in 1897, after he had played Othello. Stanislavski was well aware of the deficiences of his performance – particularly vocal – but he was not prepared to accept criticism of its being too 'modern' and insufficiently 'Shakespearian'. Where, ten years

[1] MLIA pp. 162–4.
[2] MLIA p. 163.

earlier, he had been a slave to the prevailing style, now he attacked so-called 'tradition' and advocated approaching the play in contemporary terms

> Genius is inspired by truth, by beauty, while ungifted people need a screen to hide the poverty of their talent and imagination, and so they invent tradition. They have now invented so many traditions, so many different rules, that the ordinary public can no longer understand Shakespeare and Molière has ceased to be funny....
>
> ... it is the task of our generation to banish from art outmoded tradition and routine and to give more scope to fantasy and creation. That is the only way to save art.[1];

If dead tradition was to be banished so was its inevitable companion, the acting cliché

> The actor who is not capable of the creative in art naturally is anxious to establish, once for all, the manners of theatrical interpretation – clichés. An actor played a certain role excellently; a second actor saw the performance and did not understand the genuine process of its creation but remembered the form of it. A third takes the form as an example. A fourth takes the form to be a theatrical tradition and copies it as law. With these cliché-chains one cannot reach the depth of the human soul. These chains prevent us from being guided by the most important director of the theatre – life.[2]

Stanislavski had learned to imitate life rather than other actors but he still did not understand the nature of the creative act or the inner life of the actor.

Crisis

Stanislavski had developed a technique which was purely external. He had to work from the outside in the hope that by establishing, truthfully, the external characteristics of the role he could provoke

[1] Letter to Lucien Besnard, 20 July 1897, trans. in *Stanislavski*, Progress, 1963, pp. 231–5.
[2] SD p. 399. Personal note by the translator, Miriam Goldina, recorded in 1920, during a rehearsal.

some intuitive response in himself which would lead him to the psychological aspects of the part.

His approach as a director was identical. He attempted to induce a creative mood in his actors by surrounding them with real objects, sound and lighting effects. He imposed his interpretation on every role, working endlessly, and at times ruthlessly, to get every detail exact. There was no alternative. The members of the company were, on the whole, young and inexperienced. The only way to achieve the artistic and organic unity which MXAT demanded was for everyone tó carry out to the letter the production as conceived by Stanislavski, or Nemirovich, *in advance*.

By and large this method had worked. Nemirovich could justifiably claim that the new theatre soon set the standard by which other companies were judged; that where they led others followed.[1] A triumphant tour to Berlin in 1905 gave MXAT an international reputation.

As for Stanislavski himself, his achievement in the first eight years of the theatre's existence had been truly remarkable. He had, either singly, or in collaboration with Nemirovich directed Chekhov's *Seagull* (1898), *Uncle Vanya* (1899), *Three Sisters* (1901), *Cherry Orchard* (1904), Ibsen's *Hedda Gabler* (1899), *An Enemy of the People* (1900), *The Wild Duck* (1901), *Ghosts* (1905), Gorki's *Small People* (1902), *The Lower Depths* (1902) and *Children of the Sun* (1905). He had played Trigorin (*Seagull*). Lövborg (*Hedda Gabler*) Astrov (*Uncle Vanya*), Stockmann (*Enemy of the People*), Vershinin (*Three Sisters*), Satin (*Lower Depths*) and Gaev (*Cherry Orchard*). There was no apparent reason for him not to continue along the lines he had so firmly established. None the less when he left for his summer holiday in Finland in June 1906 he was in a state of crisis, bewildered and depressed, not knowing which direction to take. He had lost all faith in himself. He felt dead on stage.[2]

This feeling of sterility had overtaken him in March of that year, during a performance – most probably of *An Enemy of the People*.[3] His muscles automatically created the external image of the character, his body mechanically repeated the actions he had

---

[1] Letter to Stanislavski, 7 August 1902 or 1903. In *Archive* No. 2, 1962.
[2] MLIA p. 458.
[3] Interview, 29 April 1912, for the magazine *Studya*.

created but there was no inner impulse, no feeling, no sense of re-creation, no *life*.

This was a particularly bitter experience for him as Stockmann had afforded him one of his rare moments of complete artistic satisfaction when creative talent and judgement had come together and his 'intuition' had functioned.

The characterisation, the physical features had sprung from his unconscious. Later he was able to identify the origin of particular elements[1] but the coming together of the performance had been spontaneous and brought with it immense pleasure. That pleasure was now gone.

There were other, fundamental problems to be resolved. What direction MXAT itself was to take? Chekhov's death, in 1904 which affected Stranislavski deeply, seemed to mark the end of an era. Relations with Nemirovich were cooling. Once inseparable collaborators, they were drawing apart, unable to agree on questions of artistic policy.

Nemirovich's production, in 1903, of *Julius Caesar* brought home to Stanislavski the limitations of his working method as an actor and of the whole approach to the interpretation of a script which he and Nemirovich had advocated. Nemirovich's production was a masterpiece of historical and archaeological reconstruction. The authenticity of the costumes, props and décor was beyond doubt; they had been thoroughly researched. Indeed, children were brought to see the play, not so much for Shakespeare but to be given some idea of what life was like in ancient Rome.

Nemirovich's historical-archaeological approach was not essentially different from Stanislasvki's own in his productions of Alexei Tolstoy's *Tsar Fyodor Ioannovich* and *The Death of Ivan the Terrible*. This time, however, Stanislavski was on the receiving end as an actor. In being subjected to his own method he experienced nothing but frustration. While he was concerned to bring out the human dilemma of Brutus' character, Nemirovich subordinated everything to his historical overview.

When the company met, as was the custom, for a final reading before the opening night everyone suddenly felt the inner reality of their roles, just as they had in Chekhov. But for Stanislavski this did not last. The whole 'operatic' apparatus of the production became oppressive to him:

[1] MLIA pp. 405–6.

Every detail of the staging, every tiny piece of the scenery seemed to me drenched in sweat; everything recalled long days of hard work; in short, instead of helping me to find the right frame of mind, all these details totally destroyed any true feelings I might experience.[1]

Only when the company went on tour to Petersburg, when everything suddenly seemed strange again did he recover any sense of truth. Yet such was Stanislavski's sense of discipline that he never questioned Nemirovich's decisions and did his best to supply what was required of him. The production was a great success. His own performance, despite spirited and loyal defence from his friends, was, on the whole, considered a failure.

The staging of Chekhov and the struggle to come to terms with his writing also raised doubts in Stanislavski's mind. It took all Nemirovich's powers of persuasion, all the brilliance of his literary analysis to convince his colleague to include *The Seagull* in the repertoire. Like many others, Stanislavski was initially disconcerted by the lack of 'action', the absence of opportunities for production effects. In fact, as he himself admitted, he planned the production without really understanding the play.[2] He penetrated beneath the surface of Chekhov's work only slowly and with difficulty. Yet when Nemirovich received the production copy he recognised the scope of Stanislavski's achievement and its originality.

It was precisely because he had to dig, probe beneath the surface, that Chekhov's scripts were so crucial to Stanislavski's development. Chekhov either could not or would not explain or expand on what he had written. He insisted that everything necessary was contained in the text. At most he would throw out a cryptic comment, pregnant with nuances. Typical is his comment to Stanislavski on his performance as Trigorin in *The Seagull*. After congratulating him he said: 'It was wonderful. Only you need torn shoes and check trousers.'[3] Stanislavski was disconcerted. He had played Trigorin as a dandy in a beautiful white suit. A year later he realised the truth of Chekhov's comment. He had opted for the conventional image of a successful, if not great, writer. But he had missed the point. It was fundamental to Nina's character that she should fall in love with a second-rate, seedy author, whom she

[1] SS Vol. I, pp. 425–6.
[2] MLIA p. 352.
[3] MLIA p. 358.

transformed, in imagination to a glamorous figure. Two adjacent photographs in the MXAT Museum show the transformation which Stanislavski's performance underwent.

Yet where in the script could he have found, in precise terms, Chekhov's image of Trigorin? Not only he but also Nemirovich, who claimed a much more profound understanding of Chekhov, had failed to detect it. How was one to approach an author who expected you to infer that Uncle Vanya was dressed, not in great boots and untidy clothes like a country farmer, but in an elegant suit on the basis of a single reference to his fine silk ties?

Experiences like these brought the whole nature of the script into question. What was the significance of the words on the page? If they did not contain the total meaning, where did the meaning lie? How was the actor to penetrate it? The response to this problem resulted in the notion of the *sub-text*.

Experiment

Stanislavski felt a constant need to move forward. His fear was stagnation. The moment when what had been fresh and new became routine and mechanical he would strike out in a new direction. He felt that MXAT was in danger of developing a rigid house style. Certain features of its productions, notably the pauses, had become sufficiently notorious for them to be satirised in Moscow cabarets. There was a danger of becoming locked in a dead naturalism. The time had come to expand the repertoire and grapple with new problems.

In 1905 he founded a Studio where young actors could experiment with new ideas and new methods.[1] He put the young Meyerhold in charge. Meyerhold had left MXAT in 1902, after playing Konstantin in *The Seagull*. Meeting him again Stanislavski found him full of ideas, confident and articulate in a way which he himself was not. Realism, authentic detail were dead; the time had come for the unreal, for dreams and visions.[2] Stanislavski was sympathetic. He had already ventured into Symbolism, attempting productions of Maeterlinck.

Having gathered a group of young actors together he gave

---

[1] The Studio on Povarskaya, not to be confused with the First Studio of 1912.
[2] MLIA p. 434.

Having gathered a group of young actors together he gave Meyerhold his head. The company spent the summer rehearsing at Pushkino where the original MXAT company had worked. In the autumn Stanislavski was shown some short extracts from the repertoire that had been chosen: Maeterlinck's *The Death of Tintagiles*, Hauptmann's *Schluck und Jau* and a number of one-acters. He was sufficiently impressed by the display to take a large 700-seat theatre on Povarskaya Street which was temporarily dark. The performance was a bitter disappointment.[1]

The young cast lacked the experience and technique necessary to carry a full-length play, adequate though they had appeared in excerpts. What came through was a clever director, manipulating an inexperienced cast, attempting to stage his ideas. But not even that came off. Meyerhold could only

> demonstrate his ideas, principles, researches, ingenuities but there was nothing that would give life to them. And without that, all the interesting plans of the stage director turned into dry theory, into a scientific formula that caused no inner reaction in the spectator.[2]

Stanislavski, at that time the master of manipulating the actor, of hiding a company's deficiencies under a wealth of ingenious detail, had once more been shown the negative side of his practice.

Having come to a dead end, for the moment at least, in his own acting, having seen his attempts to widen the repertoire and foster new acting techniques fail, he left for Finland with two questions as yet only vaguely formulated in his mind: how could an actor's creativity be stimulated and kept alive; how could a production be centred on that creative energy?[3] He realised that somewhere in the jumble of his experience lay the answers, truths which he had known for a long time.

> I had acquired through my experiences as an actor a rag-bag of material on theatrical technique. Everything had been thrown in, willy-nilly, no system.... There was a need to create some order, to sort out the material, examine it, assess it and, so to speak, place it on mental shelves. Rough matter had to be worked and polished and lain as the foundation stones of our art.[4]

[1] MLIA p. 437.
[2] Ibid.
[3] MLIA p. 438.
[4] SS Vol. 1, p. 285.

Sitting on a rock[1] he began to take stock. He reflected on what had gone wrong with his performance as Stockmann. From there he went on to review his entire career, every part he had ever played. To help him he had his Notebooks, all the impressions and reflections he had gathered together for more than twenty-five years.

He returned to his first question, one he had posed when he was only fourteen: what was it that great, intuitive actors, like Salvini, Chaliapin and Duse, possessed, what special quality? It was a gift from the gods and not available on demand.[2] These moments of 'intuition' or 'inspiration' were an everyday occurrence for actors of genius. For the less favoured they happened, as it were, on Sundays and for the second rate only on high days and holidays.

What is the actor's state? An unnatural and impossible one. Faced with blazing footlights and an audience of a thousand all an actor can do is ape, imitate, pretend, never really living or experiencing emotion. This he had known for a long time but his perception had been purely intellectual. Now he felt it with his whole being and that total, lived experience of an idea was, as he was often to repeat, the only knowledge of any value to an actor.

Imagine that you have been put on show in a very high place, in Red Square, in front of a hundred thousand people. Next to you they have put a woman, perhaps someone you have never met before. You have been ordered to fall in love with her, publicly, so deeply, in fact, that you go out of your mind and commit suicide. But there's very little of the lover about you. You are embarrassed. A hundred thousand pairs of eyes are fixed on you, waiting for you to make them cry, a hundred thousand hearts are waiting to be moved by your ideal, passionate, selfless love, because that's what they have paid for and that's what they have the right to expect. Of course, they want to hear everything you say and you have to yell your words of love, words which, in life, you would whisper to a woman close to. Everyone must see you, everyone must understand you and so you must gear your gestures and your movements to the people furthest away from you. Can you, in such conditions, think about love? Can you, indeed, experience love and the feelings love

[1] The 'bench' of the American edition becomes a 'rock' in the Russian edition.
[2] MLIA p. 461

implies? All you can do is stretch and strain, use all your efforts in a futile attempt to reach an impossible end.[1]

The actor is a being split down the middle. On one side a mind full of everyday cares, concerns and irritations, with a living to earn; on the other a body which is called on to express grand passions, heroic sentiments and evoke the whole realm of the unconscious.[2] This dichotomy is a daily experience; the actor's life has nothing to do with his profession. But because he must, somehow, produce an effect on the audience he falls back on the tricks of the trade, the stock gestures, the well-tried intonations, the whole battery of signs and signals which provide a conventional representation of emotion without actually embodying it. So the passionate lover rolls his eyes and clasps his hand to his heart, keeping up a continuous flow of sound and movement without a moment for thought or reflection.

How can this dilemma be resolved. How can this 'actor's state' be replaced by the 'creative state' which actors of genius possess? If this state comes *naturally* to the great actor then it must lie within every actor's nature to achieve it in some measure.

From the moment that it is given to men of genius to know the creative state by nature it is possible that ordinary people may get somewhere near it after much work on themselves, even if they don't achieve it in its fullest, highest measure but only partially. Of course, this will not turn an averagely talented man into a genius but will help him to approach something resembling it.[3]

Every actor has some moments of genuine creation. How could these moments be made to happen more frequently? Were there technical means of producing the creative state. Could 'inspiration' be encouraged or induced? Could the element of chance in building a performance, which had so often worried Stanislavski himself, be reduced? Was there, in fact, a grammar of acting which could be learned?

As early as 1889, in his Notebooks, Stanislavski had spoken of a 'grammar' of acting, an ABC which everyone could master. If

[1] SS Vol. 1, p. 298.
[2] SS Vol. 1, p. 299.
[3] SS Vol. 1, p. 130.

grammar is broadly understood as a system which defines the different functions and establishes the rules by which these functions combine and operate, could not something analagous apply to acting?

No language can, of course, be learned at one go.

> If [the creative state] cannot be mastered all at once, can it not be achieved bit by bit, that is to say, by constructing the whole from its parts?[1]

Each of the parts could then be taken separately and worked on through a series of exercises. The first task therefore was to define the parts.

Despite the somewhat romantic picture which Stanislavski gives of himself, sitting on a rock overlooking the sea, meditating on his career, he worked extremely hard throughout the whole of June and July. According to his wife Lilina:

> He is happy to find that the northern climate and air agree with him. But, between ourselves, our time has been spent very strangely. He doesn't go out walking, still less does he take fresh air. He sits in a half-darkened room, writing and smoking the whole day. He seems to be writing very interesting things, the title, A Draft Manual on Dramatic Art.[2]

Serious work on what was later to become the System has thus begun.[3] The basic problems had been formulated if still only in tentative form.

A fundamental shift had taken place in Stanislavski's thinking during those two months. Acting was no longer thought of as *imitation* but as *process*. It was no longer a question of purely external control, of technique, of skilfully reproducing a facsmile of experience but of creating and conveying inner life, a sense of *being*, fresh each time.

Stanislavski recognised the unconscious nature of the creative moment. But the unconscious is not susceptible to command; dreams cannot be made to measure. Only nature can create. The task then was to find ways for the actor to work with and through nature. By creating organic links between the actor's own per-

[1] SS Vol. 1, p. 300.
[2] Letter to Olga Knipper-Chekhova, quoted in *Zhizn i Tvorchestvo K. S. Stanislavskvo*, Vol. 2, Moscow, 1971, pp. 32–3.
[3] The term 'System' was first employed in 1909.

sonality and the character he was playing, the damaging rift between
the actor as human being and as performer could be healed.
Conscious activity in preparing and rehearsing a role needed to
be coherent and so organised as to create the conditions in which
spontaneous, intuitive creation could occur. That is the sole purpose of the System.

Study

Stanislavski began a period of study. There was, however, no existing body of knowledge on which he could draw. The creative
process was not an object of scientific study at the beginning of the
century. Psychology as a discipline was still in its infancy, as were
linguistics and the nature of speech-acts. He had to rely, therefore,
on the analysis of his own day-to-day activity, to seek corroboration
of his findings, where possible, in whatever relevant scientific
studies were available. He could then attempt to draw general
conclusions. He adopted two strategies; first, close observation of
himself and his colleagues in rehearsal and of major artists, both
Russian and foreign, in performance: second, readings in contemporary psychology. Of great importance in his reading was
Ribot's *Problèmes de Psychologie Affective* from which he learned
the notion of affective memory, later to be developed into Emotion
Memory.[1] Other works of Ribot to be found in his library
were *Les Maladies de la Volonté*, *Psychologie de l'Attention*, *Les
Maladies de la Mémoire*, *L'Évolution des Idées Générales*, and *La
Logique des Sentiments*.

Ribot provided Stanislavski with a key to unlock the actor's unconscious. According to his theories, the nervous system bears the
traces of all previous experiences. They are recorded in the mind,
although not always available. An immediate stimulus – a touch,
a sound, a smell – can trigger off the memory. It is possible
to recreate past events, to relive past emotions, vividly. Not only
that; similar experiences tend to merge. The memory of a particular
incident can evoke memories of similar incidents, similar feelings.
Experiences of love, hate, envy, fear come together, they are dis-
tilled so that an individual can experience an overwhelming emotion
apparently unrelated to any particular event.

Stanislavski realised that this faculty of vivid recall – dependent,

[1] AAP Chap. IX.

in life, on chance – could be harnessed to the creation of performance. If the actor could define the emotion that was required of him at any given moment and then stimulate analogous feeling from his own experience then his interpretation could attain a new level of reality and the gap between the actor as individual and the actor as performer could be bridged. The actor and the character would become one.

Great actors at work

Side by side with his reading Stanislavski continued his practical observations. As he watched artists like Salvini, Chaliapin, Duse and Ermolova he was struck once more by the degree of relaxation they achieved, the flow and response of the body to inner impulses. His experience as a director enabled him to understand and identify with them, to feel what they felt.[1]

He tried to achieve a similar state of relaxation during his own performances and when he succeeded he felt liberated, like a prisoner who had been released from his chains. But the feeling was secondhand, not directly experienced as an actor but mediated through his experience as a director. What was more, none of his fellow actors noticed any difference in his performance. He came to the conclusion that what was important was not the physical changes themselves but the mental attitude which produced them. While he was monitoring his physical state during a performance his concentration was on himself and what he was doing, not on the audience or the frightening black hole out front.[1] Moreover, the actor who focuses entirely on the stage action is more likely to produce active participation in the audience. They no longer sit back in their seats, waiting to be 'entertained'; they are drawn to watch more closely and understand.

With the progress of time this faculty of concentration was itself broken down into smaller elements – public solitude, the circle of attention, orientation – for which special exercises were developed. These were finally incorporated into *An Actor Prepares*.

The second major quality which he observed in great actors was the capacity for *belief*, to inhabit the universe created by the stage. His experience in *Julius Caesar* had shown just how

[1] SS Vol. 1, p. 301.
[2] SS Vol. 1, p. 301. MLIA p. 464.

difficult that, at times, could be. What happens in the theatre is not real in the sense that everyday life as experienced is real. How then can it be believed? On the one hand there is the injunction to be 'truthful', to draw material from living models and not from theatrical stereotypes; on the other hand there is the patent unreality of everything around you.

> What kind of truth can this be, when all on the stage is a lie, an imitation, scenery, cardboard, paint, make-up, wooden goblets, swords and spears. Is all this truth?[1]

In attempting to resolve this dilemma Stanislavski returned to the fundamental question of the purpose of his art.

> Why do we act on the stage? For what reason do we tread the boards?[2]

His answer, as always, is that we are there to present the truth of human actions and decision and feelings. The sets, the costumes, the props become, as it were, the pretext for an argument, presented in terms of dramatic action. We must, quite simply, *make believe*.

> All this scenery, props, make-up, costumes, the public nature of the creative moment – it's all lies. I know that, but what have they to do with me? Things are not important... But... *if* everything around me on stage *were* true....[3]

Then it would be possible to create a character which was based on a logical sequence of feelings and a logical series of actions, a characterisation which could be believed by actor and audience alike. The magic 'If' opens the way to the creative process.[4] Stanislavski took a phrase of Pushkin's and adapted it to his own art

> 'Sincerity of emotions, feelings that seem true in the given circumstances – that is what we ask of a dramatist.'
> I add from myself that it is exactly what we ask of an actor.[5]

The truthful, creative actor is one who can use the magic 'If', who can believe in the 'given circumstances' no matter how unlikely, no matter how fantastic. A child believes in the real existence

[1] MLIA p. 465.
[2] SS Vol. 1, p. 304.
[3] *Ibid.*
[4] AAP Chap. VIII.
[5] AAP p. 50.

of its doll.[1] Truthful acting arises similarly from the actor's capacity to transform the conventions of the play and even crude theatrical lies into an artistic reality, through his own ability to make believe. The sense of truth lies in the actor's imagination, childlike simplicity, openness and sensitivity

> All these qualities, taken together, I shall call the *feeling of truth*.[2]

Stanislavski did not accept the mere transposition of the elements of everyday life, unaltered, onto the stage, as truthful acting.

> What does it really mean to be truthful on the stage?...
> Does it mean that you conduct yourself as you do in ordinary life? Not at all. Truthfulness in those terms would be sheer triviality...[3]
> Scenic truth is not like truth in life; it is peculiar to itself.[4]

Conventions and truth

This brought Stanislavski to the whole question of theatrical convention. Theatre is convention. Theatricality, in its best sense, is everything which helps the actor's performance and the play itself. Conventions which help the creative process are good conventions. The life portrayed on stage

> must be convincing. It cannot flow amid palpable lies and deception. The lie must become or seem to be truth on the stage in order to be convincing...
>
> The production of the stage director and the playing of the actors may be realistic, conventionalised, modernistic, expressionistic, futuristic – it is all the same as long as they are convincing, that is truthful or truth-like; beautiful, that is artistic; uplifted and creating the true life of the human spirit without which there can be no art.
>
> Convention which does not fulfil these requirements must be branded as bad convention.[5]

[1] MLIA p.466.
[2] MLIA p. 467.
[3] SL p. 20.
[4] MLIA p. 466.
[5] MLIA pp. 486–7.

The actor at the centre

The centre of a production had shifted decisively from the director to the actor, who was no longer expected to conform to a predetermined pattern. The performance was to be created out of his own resources. This did not mean that the production depended on the whims and emotional caprices of the cast. Given increased responsibility actors had to develop disciplines – physical, emotional, intellectual – which would enable them to put their talents at the service of the play and its meaning. As far as Stanislavski himself was concerned it meant that he changed, as Nemirovich accurately observed, from a director to a teacher, mentor and guide.

like all earlier 18th casting

Trying new methods

This transformation, however, did not take place overnight. He was to learn how difficult the application of his ideas could be. On his return from Finland he began work on a production of Knut Hamsun's *Drama of Life*. The play was abstract, symbolic, unreal. Stanislavski seized what seemed like an ideal opportunity to strip away all gestures, all physical action and to concentrate on the 'inner state' of the actors. All the rest, he believed, would follow – almost by magic.

The result was the opposite of what he had intended; not the release of creative energy, the relaxation, the freedom he had imagined but tension, strain and frustration. Going one day into one of his assistant's rehearsals he found

A tragedian, bathed in sweat, rolling on the ground and roaring with every appearance of passion he could drag out of himself, with my assistant astride his back, yelling at the top of voice and pushing him with all his might: 'More! More! Go on! Louder!'... And to think that not so long before I had accused an assistant director of treating an actor like a horse that cannot shift its load.
– 'More, more, louder,' the assistant continued, spurring the tragedian on, 'Life, feeling! Feeling!'[1]

[1] SS Vol. 1, p. 310. A slightly different version appears in MLIA p. 475.

The whole cast went through much the same

> Each actor squeezed out of himself the passion that he was ordered to create...[1]

As a result the play was forgotten. The actors worked separately. There was no organic communication among them. The production itself was a success, provoking strong public reaction for and against, although opinion divided on political rather than artistic lines. In Stanislavski's view, however, the actors had gone backwards not forwards. Once again they had been pawns in the service of an idea, a concept.

His next production, Andreyev's *Life of Man*, was no better. Its success arose not from the actors' art but from its production values. The insights which had been achieved in Finland were not bearing fruit. The 'creative state' remained as elusive as ever.

Training

It seems evident that initially Stanislavski saw his new approach as essentially a change of rehearsal method. What he had under-estimated was the difficulty for actors to follow his lead. If much in his life had prepared him for this new departure other people had not shared his experience, or, if they had, they had not reached his level of consciousness.

Stanislavski was thus led, inevitably, to the notion of continuous training.

> After *The Drama of Life* I was in a state of total despair. It seemed that all the laboratory work I had undertaken, which might have set me on the road to a new art, had come to nothing; I was once more in a blind alley, unable to see any way out. I had to live many days and even months troubled by doubt before I understood a truth I had in fact known a long time, namely that in our profession everything must become habitual, so that the new is transformed into something organically our own, into second nature. Only when that has happened can we use what is new without thinking of the mechanics of it. The same thing applies to the *creative state*, which will only save the actor once it has become his normal, natural and only state. Otherwise the actor will only copy the

[1] MLIA p. 475.

outward forms of radical forward-thinking art, without inner justification, and he will not even realise what he is doing.[1]

If the creative state was to become second nature the actor must condition himself. This meant daily exercises. No less than the dancer or the athlete the actor must keep himself on form.

Circumstances did not allow Stanislavski to develop his methods other than during rehearsals, in a rather *ad hoc* manner, for some years. None the less the need for a coherent, systematic approach to work, on a daily basis, became more and more apparent, particularly when training young actors.

First drafts

In the meantime work went on, writing down what was still called the 'grammar'. Apart from the difficulty of isolating and defining the elements of that grammar, there was the problem of finding a vocabulary. There was no agreed terminology. Stanislavski had received a fairly advanced musical training and he deplored the fact that the actor, unlike the musician, had no precise system of notation, no agreed language in which to discuss his problems and intentions.

> How lucky to have at one's disposal bars, pauses, a metronome, a tuning fork, harmony, counterpoint, properly worked-out exercises to develop technique, a vocabulary in which to describe artistic concepts, to understand creative problems and experiences. Music has long since recognised the importance of such vocabulary. Music can rely on recognised basic rules and not, like us, on pot-luck[2]

The Stanislavski Archives contain a series of drafts, dating from 1907: *Reference Book for the Dramatic Actor; Practical Information and Good Advice for Beginners and Students of Dramatic Art; Draft of a Popular Manual of Dramatic Art*, etc. A terminology began to emerge, although it was by no means stable. Changes were introduced over the next four years. However, if the vocabulary was still fluctuating the elements which went to make up the creative state were becoming clearer.

[1] SS Vol. 1, pp. 310–311.
[2] SS Vol. 1, pp. 369–370.

The Notebooks for 1908 contain a series of entries, grouped under specific headings – muscular relaxation, circle of attention, belief, dramatic inventiveness, feelings.[1] His work was sufficiently advanced for him to be able to announce in his address, celebrating the tenth anniversary of MXAT that henceforth the work of the company, following in the tradition of Shchepkin, would be based on clear, simple psychological and physiological laws.

Two documents from 1909 indicate the stage his ideas had reached. On March 8 he delivered a paper at a theatrical conference. In it he stated that the actor's art consisted of six principal processes:

> *In the first preparatory process of the 'will'* the actor prepares himself for future creation. He gets to know the author's work, he becomes enthusiastic or makes himself enthusiastic about it and so arouses his creative gifts, *i.e.* stimulates the desire to create;
>
> *In the second process, 'searching'*, he looks within himself and outside himself for the psychological material needed for creation;
>
> *In the third process, 'experience'*, the actor creates *invisibly, for himself*. He creates in his dreams the inner and outer image of the character he is to portray . . . he must adapt himself to this alien life and feel it as though it were his own . . .;
>
> *In the fourth process, 'physicalizing'*, the actor creates *visibly, for himself*;
>
> *In the fifth processs, 'synthesis'*, the actor must *bring together* to a point of total synthesis the process of 'experience' and the process of 'physicalization'. These two processes must proceed simultaneously, start together, help and develop each other;
>
> *The sixth process* is that of the effect on the audience.[2]

From June of the same year comes an outline for an article on the new system. It lists the various elements which go to make up the creative state, such as relaxation, experience and emotion memory, although the terminology is not always final.[3]

By the summer of 1910 Stanislavski was so full of ideas he

[1] KSA Nos. 264, 271.
[2] KSA No. 257.
[3] KSA No. 625.

could scarcely get them down on paper fast enough. Writing to Olga Sulerzhitska in August he told her

> This is my time of harvest. For two months, in my mind, I planted the seeds of ideas and problems concerning the System. They grew with difficulty and would not let me sleep but now the first shoots appear – and I can't get down on paper everything that is springing up and requires even approximate verbal definition. If I don't manage to get it down I shall have to begin all over again next year, because all this is so unclear, so quickly forgotten and next year, just as here, now, in the Caucasus, I shall not be able to get down everything that has come to fruition...[1]

By now Stanislavski was working in greater depth and detail. The two manuscripts of 1909 contain in essence, the concepts which were to be worked out during the rest of his career.

First success of the new system

Stanislavski's new found energy and confidence were in no small measure due to the fact that he had at last managed to prove to himself and his colleagues that his new ideas worked *theatrically*. His concern was still the actor's creativity and the 'inner state', but he had succeeded in going far beyond his experiments in *The Drama of Life*. Turgenev's *A Month in the Country*, which he directed in 1908, was the ideal script on which to work. No play is more dependent on minute, inner shifts of mood and feeling. There is virtually no external action and no opportunity for director's effects. Stanislavski responded to this opportunity. He asked for simple sets and allowed the minimum of gesture and movement:

> A bench or a sofa to which people go to sit and talk – no sounds, no details, no minutiae. Everything depends on lived experience and the voices. The whole play intertwines the emotions and feelings of author and actor. How can you write down the elusive means by which a director works with actors? It's a sort of hypnosis based on the psychological state of actors at work, on knowledge of their character, their faults. In this

play, as in all others, this work and *only this* is essential and worthy of attention.[1]

This is a far cry from the prescriptive production plans of the *Seagull* but it marks Stanislavski's definitive position. Writing to Sergei Balukhaty in February 1925, he emphasised the importance of the change:

> Bear in mind that the *mises en scène* of the *Seagull* were made by the old, now completely rejected methods of imposing one's personal emotions on the actor, and not by the new method of studying the actor beforehand – his capacities, the material of his part, before creating the appropriate *mise en scène*. In other words, the method of the old *mises en scène* belongs to the despotic director, against whom I now battle, while the new *mises en scène* are made by directors who depend upon the actor.[2]

As far as *A Month in the Country* was concerned, he stated quite bluntly: 'There is no *mise en scène* of any kind.'[3]

As well as directing he undertook the demanding role of Rakitin. He was therefore able to experience the problems of getting the play on from two distinct but related view-points.

> Stanislavski the actor... knew only too well the problems that Stanislavski the stage director had placed before him.[4]

This time he decided to trust the actor in himself and not the director.[5]

He proceeded as follows. First the play was broken down, as usual, into segments. Each segment was then described in terms of the characters' psychology and the particular state they were in at a given moment. In each segment therefore the actor had a specific psychological goal to attain. For every action that was planned there was an inner justification, springing from the total life of the character. The life of a character is not, of course,

[1] SS Vol. 7, p. 451, Letter No. 337.
[2] SS Vol. 8, p. 102, Letter No. 74. Translation in *Stanislavski*, Progress, 1963, p. 251.
[3] SS Vol. 1, Letter No. 337.
[4] MLIA p. 543.
[5] MLIA p. 544.

shown in its entirety during the course of a play, which is necessarily selective. The actor must therefore supplement the script with his own imagination, create the moments between the scenes, the flow and continuity of the character's life. No moment of stage action is static. It is part of a dynamic process. The sequence of psychological states reveals the total character which is, in turn, determined by the overall conception of the play.

The procedures which Stanislavski employed in a systematic manner for the first time later became known as *units and objectives*, *sub-text*, the *through-line of action* and the *superobjective*.

As far as rehearsals were concerned Stanislavski adopted his usual practice of a lengthy period of readings round the table during which the play was analysed. This initial stage took two months. Readings were, for the first time, interspersed with exercises to develop concentration, the circle of attention, and the appropriate psychological states. The theory of emotion memory was tested out. Actors were required to explore their own living experience in order to find equivalents for the feelings experienced by the characters. The whole psychological plan was then realised, physically.

Stanislavski broke with established custom by telling the members of the company that they would not be required, as was normal, to attend all the rehearsals. He isolated his cast for more than four months. So concerned was he with the intimate, inward nature of the play that he worked in the small rehearsal theatre rather than on the main stage, sub-dividing it still further into even smaller spaces. Exterior action, movement, gesture were reduced to almost nothing. The actors were required to 'radiate' their feelings, to do everything through the eyes, by tiny changes of tone and inflection, to 'commune' with each other. Here Stanislavski used notions drawn from Yoga. The text was rarely spoken out loud. It was whispered, held back. Cuts were made in the longer speeches and the omitted sections were used as sub sub-text.

> How to lay bare the actor's soul so that it becomes visible and comprehensible to the audience?...What we need is a kind of invisible radiation of feeling and creative will – eyes, facial expression, fleeting, elusive tones of voice, psychological pauses...We had once more to return to immobility, absence of gestures, we had to get rid of all superflous movement; we had to cut down, no, cut out entirely all director's moves

and leave the actors motionless on their chairs; let them speak, think and communicate their suffering to the thousands in the audience.[1]

Stanislavski had come to believe that the more intense the communication among the actors on stage, the clearer the action would be and the more involved the audience could become. The cast was, as Gogol had recommended, to *transmit* their feelings, not present them.[2]

The production was a success, and Stanislavski scored a personal triumph with his interpretation of Rakitin. The new method of working had, however, revealed another problem.

Reading the play

The shift of responsibility from the dictator-director, who alone holds the secret of the interpretation, to the creative performer means that the actor needs much more sophisticated reading skills. He must be able to break down the play into its constituent parts, into *units and objectives* but at the same time keep a broader view of the coherence of his role – the *through-line of action* – and the significance of the play as a whole – the *super-objective*.

Stanislavski's own response to *A Month in the Country* had been immediate: it was a world that was familiar to him. Other members of the company experienced much greater difficulty and he realised that they lacked a technique, or method, of reading.

Actor's reading is of a particular kind. It is not the reading of the literary critic. It is not objectively analytical. It is a form of reading which is designed to stimulate enthusiasm, evoke commitment and stir the imagination. It is the first attempt to activate the unconscious. It becomes therefore a disciplined interchange between the elements of the script and the personal responses and images which the actor brings to it. The investigation of the script, the clear understanding of its nature and its relation to an actor's own experience is the primary process in rehearsal from which all others follow.

Just as the creative state can be broken down into its elements so can the process of reading. For those who do not have an immediate, instinctive and appropriate response to the script there is a step by step procedure. Stanislavski compared the process

[1] SS Vol. 1, p. 326.
[2] See above.

to a train journey. There are those, the geniuses, who speed from terminus to terminus; others who have to stop at intermediate stations and explore the surrounding countryside: yet others halt at whistle-stops.[1] Everyone has the same journey to go, the difference is the number of stages the journey takes.

Stanislavski set about studying the particular problems of script reading by analysing his own practice. The Archives contain a manuscript from the period 1909–11, a draft chapter and another dated 1915, entitled *The History of a Character*. Great emphasis is placed on the use of '*Emotion Memory*' to bring the script alive and motivate its elements. Stanislavski describes three stages by which an actor gets into a part. First he must clearly reconstruct in his mind all the experiences delineated in the text and which he has filled out with his own imagination, down to the smallest detail. Second he must identify with the character and with the decor which surrounds him. Third comes the creation of specific objectives which will enable him to play the through-line of the work and the character. In his notes for the rehearsals of *The Village of Stepanchikovo* (1916) he emphasises the importance of the first approach to the work, particularly the first reading. What he understands by preliminary reading is outlined in the first chapter of *Creating A Role*, which he drafted between 1916 and 1920.[2] It takes place on various levels.

1. The level of facts; what happens, the events, incidents which constitute the external action and give life to the characters' emotions and states of feeling.
2. The social level: how the external action is determined by social and historical circumstance.
3. The literary level: the distinctive features of the author's style.
4. The aesthetic level: how the material in the script connects with the other arts (visual, musical).

Reading of this kind presupposes a high level of education and culture. Stanislavski never pretended it could be otherwise. Writing to an aspiring young actor in 1901 he made no secret of the amount of reading and study the boy would have to undertake before he would be accepted for training or could begin to approach the major works of the contemporary repertoire.[3] Study of the

[1] Notebooks 1927–8. Quoted by Maria Knebel in *K. Voprosou o Metodye Deistvennovo Analiza*, in *Voprosi Teatralnovo Iskousstva*, Moscow, 1978.
[2] CAR pp. 12–18.
[3] SL pp. 27–28.

script would lead to further research, to visits to museums, art galleries etc., to bring the world of the play alive.

A new status for the text

In pursuing his enquiries Stanislavski arrived at conclusions which, although common currency now, were, at the time, original. First was the realisation that dialogue is situational. The meaning of the words spoken depends not merely on their information content but on the situation in which they occur; it depends on the personal attitudes of the speaker, the personal position of the recipient, the relationship between the two and the context in which the exchange takes place. The exchange in the theatre moreover has a double context, since it is intended to be understood not only by the participants but by third parties, the audience.

Such a notion redefines the status of the text. The printed words do not contain the full meaning, as in purely literary forms. They depend on what lies beneath them, on the sub-text. The script ceases to be an art-form based on verbal organisation, like a poem or a novel, and becomes the pretext and context for an activity.

Acting is no longer imitation. The task is not to find intonations and gestures which conform to the features of the script, or to match acting conventions with literary conventions. The script loses its status as an object 'out there' to be copied. It is drawn into the creative process and is transformed by it. The creative actor fills out the script with his own experience. The artistic restructuring of the raw material of his life is controlled by the writing. The final performance is a synthesis of both. Without this process of interaction and transformation there is only literary theatre, cold dead theatre.[1]

For a short while Stanislavski even considered a new status for the writer. In 1911 both he and Gorki were convalescing in Capri. He showed Gorki his draft notes on the System. Then the two men moved on to much broader discussions. They explored the idea of a writer working with a company and creating a play out of group improvisation. It is not certain whose idea this was initially. Stanislavski certainly discussed it on his return to Moscow and Gorki returned to the subject in a letter the following year.

[1] SL 'The Theatre in which the Playwright is Paramount', pp. 171–4.

Nothing came of it but ultimately their joint experience bore fruit in the work of the First Studio, founded in 1914, where improvisation became an essential feature of its training.

Continued personal success as an actor provided Stanislavski with additional confirmation of the validity of his ideas. In 1910 he played the Old General in Ostrovski's *Even a Wise Man Stumbles*. So complete was the fusion between his own personality and the character that a close friend, seeing him in the wings, could not recognise him.[1] What had been an accident in *An Enemy of the People* had now become ordered practice thanks to the System.

By 1911 the System existed in a primitive form, almost exclusively as a psycho-technique. Nemirovich announced that it was to be officially adopted by MXAT as a working method and in 1912 the First Studio was founded for the purpose of training young actors. Stanislavski himself did not have time to take charge of the Studio. It was therefore put into the hands of his friend and collaborator Sulerzhitsky. This would seem to imply that the System was sufficiently well formulated for someone else to be able to teach it.

An actor must know how to speak

It was typical of Stanislavski that, at the very moment when he was preoccupied with the inner state of the actor and with his psycho-technique, he should be discussing a joint project with Gordon Craig. No one could have been more dissimilar to Stanislavski than Craig, with his notion of the actor as a manipulatable object, an *Übermarionette*. Stanislavski was concerned to demonstrate that his System was based on natural laws and therefore could be applied to any kind of script. What he wished to avoid was the identification of this work with plays which could be classed, broadly, as 'naturalistic'. It was essential for the System to prove its worth in the classical repertoire. In the event the Craig production of *Hamlet* was inconclusive, mainly for technical and design reasons.

It was two other works from the classical repertoire, Pushkin's *Mozart and Salieri* (1914) and Byron's *Cain* (1920) which revealed

[1] Gurevich, L., in *O Stanislavskom* p. 126 (Moscow 1948).

inadequacies in the System as it stood. In the Pushkin play Stanislavski was cast as Salieri. He was a failure. His vocal technique was inadequate to match and express the inner life of the role. He lacked expressive range and flexibility. He lived the part but the audience had no way of sharing the experience. In his attempts to convey the inner state he dragged out the lines with such heavy pauses that the words came out practically one by one. By the time he came to the end of the sentence everyone had forgotten what the beginning was about. The quality of his voice steadily deteriorated. In an attempt to make it more melodious, he resorted to a time-honoured set of tricks. Pushkin's finely finely-wrought verse was totally lost.

Stanislavski's failure in *Othello* in 1896 had also been due to vocal deficiencies. He had never mastered the art of speaking verse.

> The more I listened to my own voice and diction the more I realised that it was not the first time I had spoken verse badly. I had always spoken on stage like that. I blushed for shame over the past. I would have loved to have called it back so as to wipe out the trace of what I had left. Imagine a singer who has been successful all his life and who suddenly discovers, as he approaches old age, that he has always sung out of tune. At first he doesn't want to believe it. He goes to the piano every other minute to check his voice, to verify a phrase, and learns for certain that he is a quarter of a tone down or a semi-tone up. That is exactly what happened to me at that time.
>
> Worst of all, looking back, I understood that many of my faults and previous ways of working tension, lack of control, clichés, tics, tricks, vocal mannerisms, actor's emotion – were frequently attributable to the fact that I was not master of my own voice, which alone could give me what I needed to express my inner experience...[1]

But it was no mean task to achieve a form of speech which was at once heightened and poetic but simple and noble. If he now found ordinary daily speech vulgar and impoverished, he had no time for the artificial, bombastic style of declamation to which most actors, when in doubt, resorted. He was looking for that poetic, uncluttered delivery that Shchepkin had stumbled on.

[1] SS Vol. 1, p. 368.

I understood that knowing how to speak verse simply and elegantly was itself a science, with its own laws. But I did not know them.[1]

Stanislavski turned to those scientific works which were available, among them Volkonski's *The Expressive Word* (St Petersberg, 1913) and Ushakov's *Brief Introduction to the Science of Language* (Moscow, 1913). The Notebooks contain extensive commentaries on both works and they formed the basis of his teaching for many years.

Expressive movement

The 1920 production of *Cain* revealed another area which Stanislavski had neglected in his insistence on the primacy of the inner state: expressive movement. Freedom from tension and muscular relaxation, although important in themselves, were not enough. They were the basis for more developed work. For *Cain*, Stanislavski required much greater plasticity and control from his cast, the more so since economic circumstances progressively placed more responsibility on their shoulders. The elaborate sets that had been originally planned proved too expensive. Even the simplified sets that were agreed upon could not be properly constructed because of lack of materials. The play had to be carried by the actors. While, thanks to a great deal of work, the speaking of the verse was sharp, clear and muscular, it was not matched by equal skill on the physical side. The giant statues and architectural decor, which stood behind the cast, imposed a set of visual values which threw the inadequacy of the actors into even greater relief.

A production based on three dimensions, obliging me to concentrate my attention on the actors' movements, showed me quite clearly that we not only needed good speech in the right tempo and the right rhythm but that we also needed to be able to move in rhythm. It also showed me that there are a certain number of laws which can serve as a guide. This discovery spurred me on to a whole new series of investigations.[2]

He had a number of discussions with Isadora Duncan in 1908

[1] *Ibid.*
[2] SS Vol. 1, pp. 381–2.

when she visited Moscow. He was aware that any kind of movement training for actors had to be specially constructed to develop strength, stamina and flexibility. He now turned to the work of Emile Jaques-Dalcroze (1865–1950) whose system of Eurythmics had achieved a world-wide reputation. Stanislavski by no means gave unqualified approval to Dalcroze's work, which he often found mechanical in its approach. He insisted on an inner justification for and an awareness of each movement. None the less Dalcroze provided a base, and the exercises were taught by Stanislavski's brother, Vladimir.

Tempo-rhythm

More and more Stanislavski became preoccupied with the problem of *tempo-rhythm*, both inner and outer. Within the action of the play events, emotions have a particular pulse and pattern to them. Tempo, as in music, denotes the speed of an action or a feeling – fast, slow, medium. Rhythm, internally, indicates the *intensity* with which an emotion is experienced: externally it indicates the pattern of gestures moves and actions which express the emotion. The relationship between inner and outer tempo-rhythm is extremely complex and ultimately required no less than two complete chapters in *Building A Character*.[1]

To achieve organic unity of a production demands rhythmic coherence both in the parts and in the organisation of the whole.

Stanislavski was given an opportunity to develop his ideas on the subject thanks to an invitation, in 1918, to teach acting at the Opera Studio. The presence of music with its constant changes of speed and emotional tone prompted him to certain conclusions:

Stage action, like speech, must be musical. Movement must follow a continuous line, like a note from a stringed instrument, or, when necessary, stop short like the staccato of a coloratura soprano...Movements have their legato, staccato, andante, allegro, piano and forte and so on. The tempo and the rhythm of the action must correspond to the music. Why is it that opera singers have not grasped this simple truth? Most of them sing in one rhythm, in a certain tempo, walk in another, move their arms in a third and live their emotions in a fourth. Can harmony, without which there is no music and which has a

[1] Chapters 11 and 12.

fundamental need of order, be created out of this disparity? To bring music, singing, words and action into unison it is not an external, physical tempo that is required but an internal, spiritual one. It must be felt in the sounds, in the words, in the action, in the gestures, in the moves, in the whole production.[1]

* * *

While at the Bolshoi Studio Stanislavski gave his first recorded exposition of the System in a series of lectures in which both the elements and the philosophical background are explained. These lectures were not prepared. They were, as with all Stanislavski's statements at this period, working statements for fellow professionals. There was no intention to publish them. However, one of the singers who attended these lectures, Konkordia Antarova, took copious notes. Stanislavski's sister, Zinaida tracked them down in 1938. They were edited by Mrs Gurevich and published in Moscow in 1939 and were later translated into English.[2]

By the early twenties Stanislavski had gathered all the material which was later to be embodied in *An Actor Prepares*, *Building a Character*, and *Creating A Role* but it was a number of years before he was prepared to commit the System formally to print.

---

[1] SS Vol. 1, p. 387.
[2] *Stanislavski on the Art of the Stage*, trans. Magarshack, London, Faber, 1950.

3

Writing the System

The legacy

For more than thirty years Stanislavski made notes and drafts for his 'grammar' or manual on acting. Books were projected but, with the exception of *My Life in Art*, never written.[1] There were many reasons for this. Stanislavski was always moving forward, revising and modifying his methods so that no single formulation seemed satisfactory for very long. He rebelled against the notion that his System could be codified once and for all or that it should degenerate into a set of mechanical practices, repeated without thought or feeling. He had experienced what mere lip-service could do during the period of the First Studio when many actors had adopted his terminology but continued to act essentially in the same manner as before. The vocabulary was enough. He did not wish the 'laws' he had discovered to be identified with the techniques and exercises that were used to understand and master them. If the laws were immutable the techniques were many and changing. Thus, having used methods of voice training based on the work of Volkonski for many years he abandoned them as being too rigid and liable to mechanical repetition without thought or inner justification.

He was also concerned to verify his theories through his practice and, whenever possible, to find corroboration of a more scientific kind. Even in his last years he continued to make extensive notes on books such as Sechenov's *Reflections on the Cerebral Cortex*, and on Pavlov's experiments. In 1936 he wrote to Pavlov suggesting closer discussions. Thus, while he discussed his ideas and plans enthusiastically with friends and colleagues he held back from committing himself in a definitive manner.

None the less, as he approached seventy, he felt the need to pass on his findings in some more permanent form to younger generations. He had lived through a period of extreme turmoil; he had witnessed the October Revolution and the birth of a new

[1] First published in the USA in 1924. First Russian edition 1926. See Appendix.

society; thanks to Lenin's personal support, he had survived Meyerhold's attempt to close the theatre down; he had fought what he considered the mechanism and intellectualism of the avant-garde during the twenties; he had maintained his position within the tradition of realism. The purpose of the books was to state that position as a reminder to younger generations who were moving into new areas.

> I would like, in the last years of my life to be what I really am, the man I cannot help being according to those very laws of nature by which I have worked and lived all my life in art.
> But who am I? Where and how can I find a place in this new theatre that is coming into being? Can I still, as I once did, understand all the subtle nuances of the life going on around me and everything that inspires young people?
> I fear that many of the aspirations of young people today are beyond my comprehension – biologically. One should have the courage to face that...[1]

None the less, whatever the historical differences between generations

> The process of artistic creation remains the same in its fundamental, natural laws for the actor of the new generation as for the actor of generations gone by.[2]

There must be research, there must be experiment but there must always be a return to basic laws:

> It is useful for a young man to leave the well-beaten track for a while, to turn off the highway stretching safely away into the distance to wander freely along the byways, gathering fruit and flowers, returning, arms laden with new discoveries, to the main road, ignoring his fatigue. But it would be dangerous for him to go off the main highway completely. Art has been moving along it since time immemorial. The man who does not know this eternal road is condemned to wander endlessly in ways that lead nowhere and to be lost in the maze of thickets without ever reaching the light and open country.[3]

[1] SS Vol. 1, p. 407.
[2] SS Vol.1, p. 408.
[3] *Ibid.*

Stanislavski saw himself as a gold-prospector who after years wandering through the brush finds a vein of gold and from a mass of sand and rock extracts a few tiny nuggets.

> This precious metal, fruit of a lifetime's research in art, is my 'System' – what they call my System.[1]

A sequence of books

At the end of the revised 1936 edition of *My Life In Art* Stanislavski announced his intention of publishing his System.[2] He outlined the general scheme as follows:

> My 'System' is divided into two basic parts:
> 1. The internal and external work of an actor on himself;
> 2. The internal and external work on a role. The inner work of an actor consists in perfecting a psychological technique which will enable him to put himself, when the need arises, in the creative state, which invites the coming of inspiration. The external work of an actor on himself consists in preparing his bodily apparatus to express the role physically and to translate his inner life into stage terms. Work on a role consists in studying the spiritual essence of a dramatic work, in understanding the original seed which gave it birth and life, which determines its meaning as a totality and the meaning of the individual roles which go to make it up.[3]

Stanislavski had, in fact, already worked out in greater detail how he was to proceed. In a letter to his literary collaborator Mrs Gurevich, written on 23 and 24 December 1930, he outlined a sequence of seven books which were to cover all aspects of his thinking:

1. *My Life in Art*, which had already been published and was intended to show an artist's progress from an amateur approach to knowledge of the System;
2. Work on Oneself, was to be devoted to actor training and divided into two parts, a) Experience, b) Physical Characterisation;

[1] *Ibid.*
[2] SS Vol. 1, pp. 408–9.
[3] *Ibid.*

3. Work on a Role, would deal with units, objectives, and action. The area of study would be, not scenes, extracts or exercises, but the whole play;
4. Possibly to be combined with 3, would continue discussion of work on a role, leading to the creative state in which the unconscious becomes active;
5. Building on the material of the preceding volumes this book was to be devoted to a broader discussion of the problems of performance.
6. The art of the director – whose task is to build and maintain an ensemble.
7. The problems of directing and performing in opera.[1]

The sequence of books 1–5 denotes the sequence of learning. The acquisition of the System is a step by step process, with the problems placed in a specific order. Thus, mastery of the material in the early books leads to a discussion of the broader problems of creating performances.

The books are divided into two groups – the basic grammar (Books 2 and 3) and the working method (Books 4 and 5). It is important to register this division clearly, for while Stanislavski remained constant in his definition of the basic elements, both psychological and physical, of acting, his views on their use and application were subject to radical revision. His problem was that such a revision was occurring precisely at the moment when he had committed himself to publishing a coherent exposition of his teaching. Nowhere is this better illustrated that in his constant changes of mind concerning the format of the second book, 'Work on Oneself.'

Ideally he would have liked it to consist of a single volume. He was increasingly dissatisfied with the mind-body split which was inherent in his earlier statements. The division between the imaginative preparation of a role and its physical expression was artificial and constantly negated by his own practice. He was, therefore, far from happy about dividing the Book Two into Experience and Physical Characterisation. This could only lend authority to practices he more and more regarded as mistaken. But, as he explained to Mrs Gurevich in his letter of December 1930, to have put all the material in one book would have meant more than 1200 printed pages. Reluctantly he opted for two parts.

[1] SS Vol. 8, pp. 271–2, Letter No. 222.

By 1932 he had changed his mind and was back to the idea of one book. It would have been a vast undertaking and he was pressed for time. His health was failing. In any case, the chapters on Experience were already substantially written and his new ideas were still in the early stages of development. He had, therefore, to be content with setting down his theory and practice as it stood, in the hope that he could correct and revise later, once the total scheme was complete. In the event he compromised, inserting some of his new ideas – particularly concerning physical action – which he knew, strictly speaking, belonged to a later stage.

He gave Book Two the general title *An Actor's Work on Himself*. This places the responsibility where he thought it should lie – with the actor himself. The actor is ultimately responsible for his own development; he must motivate his own work; sharpen his own awareness and critical faculties; answer for his own talent.

An Actor Prepares

The work which we know in English as *An Actor Prepares* is the first part of Book Two. Its full title in the Soviet edition is *An Actor's Work on Himself in the Creative Process of Experience*. By and large it is a summation of Stanislavski's work between 1906 and 1914, when the emphasis was on the inner process, the psycho-technique. In the scheme of the actor's development it represents the first year's work.

Outlines of the book had been ready since the early twenties. The Notebooks contain a number of provisional titles – *Diary of a Pupil*, *The Art and Psychotechnique of the Actor*, *Nature of the Actor's Creativity*, *My Theatre School*, *Stanislavski's System*. *Diary of a Pupil* is the most accurate indication of the book's final form.

Turning to the book again after completing the revisions for the first Soviet edition of *My Life in Art* (1926) Stanislavski adopted the fictional form which he was to continue to use thereafter. He himself becomes Tortsov, the teacher and his classes are described by one of his young students, Kostya.

He was by no means certain that he had made the right decision in abandoning formal exposition and it is true that some critics have found Stanislavski's masquerading, thinly disguised, as Tortsov an unnecessary device. Experience had shown Stanislavski however, that actors do not respond well to purely theoretical statements. In the early days of the System he had antagonised some of his colleagues by attempting intellectual explanation which they rejected.[1]

> You cannot talk to actors in dry, scientific language, and indeed I am myself not a man of science, so I could not do it in any case.
>
> My task is to talk to the actor in his own language, not in order to philosophise about art...but rather to open up for him in simple form the ways of a psycho-technique which is a practical necessity to him...[2]

The fictional form enabled Stanislavski to present acting problems as lived experiences and to describe exercises in action. Stanislavski is both the master, Tortsov, and the pupil, Kostya (the short version of his own first name, Konstantin). Thus, the elderly Stanislavski meets the young actor he once was. The book is a distillation of his own learning process. Kostya and his fellow pupils follow the path of discovery which Stanislavski himself took. They are first confronted with the notion of acting as process, not imitation, polarised in the opposition between the school of being and the school of representation. Thereafter they investigate the basic elements of the psycho-technique – the Magic 'If', Given Circumstances, Public Solitude, the Circle of Attention, Communion etc. By the end of the book they have explored the actor's inner processes.

Building A Character

Stanislavski entitled the second part of Book Two (which we know as *Building A Character*) *An Actor's Work on Himself in the Creative Process of Physical Characterisation*.[3] It is based on the work he did on physical and vocal technique between 1914

[1] See Harvey Pincher, *Chekov's Leading lady*, London, John Murray, 1979, pp. 181–2.
[2] SL p. 30.
[3] The Russian term 'Voploshchenye' is difficult to translate. Literally it means 'incarnation', 'embodiment'. Both terms in English, however, have irrelevant overtones. The first chapter of *Building A Character*, in Mrs Hapgood's translation, is headed 'Physical Characterisation' and this term has been adopted.

and 1920. It represents the second year of an actor's training.

Stanislavski died before work on Part Two was complete. It has therefore been editorially reconstructed.[1] The manuscripts which Stanislavski left are heavily annotated in the margins with comments like 'repetitious', heavy and incomprehensible', 'shorter, simpler'. As always there are innumerable variants. The general shape of the book, however, is clear: a series of chapters on physical and vocal technique, followed by chapters in which the inner and outer aspects of acting are drawn together. There are a number of outline plans dating from the years 1932–5.[2] In a letter to Mrs Gurevich dated 17 February 1932, he speaks of chapters on the Development of Physical Expression, Voice and Language, Characterisation, and the Creative State on the Stage. In 1935 he made a list of the order of chapters he envisaged. In order to stress the continuity with Part One, which contained fourteen chapters, he begins numbering from 15.

15. Towards a Physical Characterisation.
16. Physical Culture.
17. Diction and Singing.
18. Language.
19. Tempo-Rhythm.
20. Characterisation.
21. Control and Mastery.
22. External State on Stage.
23. General State on Stage.
24. Fundamentals of the System.
25. How to use the System.

Some elements of this outline remain constant through all future drafts and plans.

That same year Stanislavski charged G. Kristi with the task of putting the existing manuscripts in proper order.[3] The Soviet edition is based on this editorial work. The chapters are arranged in the following order (Asterisks denote chapter titles which occur in *Building A Character*; titles in square brackets are those ascribed by the Soviet editorial committee):

---

[1] See Appendix for discussion on editorial differences in Russian and English editions.
[2] KSA Nos. 68, 274, 520, 663.
[3] KSA Nos. 263, 368.

 1. Transition Towards Physical Characterisation.*
 2. Making the Body Expressive.*
      (a) [Gymnastics, acrobatics, dance, fencing.]
      (b) Plasticity of motion.
 3. Voice and Language.
 4. Perspective in Character Building.*
 5. Tempo-Rhythm.*
 6. Logic and continuity.
 7. Characterisation.
 8. Control and mastery.
 9. Stage Charm.*
 10. Towards an Ethics for the Theatre.*
 11. State of feeling on Stage.
      (a) External state.
      (b) General state.
          [Verification of the State of Feeling on Stage.]
 12. [Final Conversations.]

Parts One and Two of Volume Two, taken together, represent a complete programme of basic training for the actor.

Creating a Role

Book Three of the sequence, which we know as *Creating A Role*, bears the title, *An Actor's Work on a Role* in the Soviet edition. Here the students, having devoloped the basis of their psycho-physical technique move on from training exercises to an examination of the problems of preparing and structuring a complete performance.

This book owes even more to editorial work than *Building A Character*. Stanislavski's manuscripts are confused. There are frequent repetitions. The same idea is expressed many different ways. Sometimes pages are not even numbered. We are faced with material for a book rather than a completed work.

The three sections cover the years 1916–1937. Part One, which centres on Griboyedov's classic *Woe from Wit* consists of an incomplete manuscript some of which was probably dictated to Mrs Gurevich's daughter between 1916 and 1920. Written before Stanislavski had decided on the fictional form, it is straightforward exposition. It summarises the basic working method of MXAT at the time – textual study and research, imaginative recreation of the inner life and physical appearance of the character, followed by physical characterisation. It is a model not a statement of invariable practice. Stanislavski was, by common consent, the most inventive and stimulating of directors, immediately responsive to actors' difficulties. Faced with their needs, although he would not compromise on the elements of the System, the 'laws', he would not allow his application of the System in practice to be inhibited by anything he had written or said elsewhere. He never approached two plays in the same manner. Where necessary the stages of preparation, separated out for the purposes of explanation were telescoped or combined according to the real situation.[1]

Part Two, dealing with work on *Othello* was drafted between 1930 and 1933, and is closely related to the production plan which Stanislavski was working on at the time. Part Three, dealing with Gogol's *The Government Inspector*, dates from 1936–7 and is his only statement concerning his later ideas on working method. Taken with the Appendix *Supplement to Creating A Role*[2] it is a valuable introduction to the last phase of Stanislavski development.

Creating A Role is not only a statement of ideas on rehearsal and, notably, methods of reading but also a record of changing practice and the slow movement towards the Method of Physical Action.

Whatever their state of editorial completion the three major texts we possess on the System must all be considered provisional. Even *An Actor Prepares*, which Stanislavski did see through the press, was already being revised even as it was being printed. Stanislavski's notes indicate that he intended transferring some material within the book itself and moving other material to later volumes where it more properly belonged in the sequence as originally planned. Given Stanislavski's infinite capacity for self-criticism it is doubtful whether he would ever have considered any version as definitive.

[1] SD p. 393.
[2] CAR pp. 253–255.

The System: a diagram

The Archives contain a number of sketches which Stanislavski made
in an attempt to present the System in diagrammatic form. There
is an account towards the end of *Building A Character* of an elaborate 'visual aid' which was set up. Robert Lewis's book *Method or
Madness* also contains a diagram which he took down in Moscow in
the early thirties. The diagram which follows here is substantially
based on the one which appears in Volume 4 of the Soviet edition of
the Complete Works, supplemented with material from other
sources.

   The spine of the diagram goes from the premise of the System –
Through the Conscious to the Unconscious [1] to the reason for the
performance, the Superobjective[15], which must remain provisional until it has been verified and refined through the process of
rehearsal. The attainment of the Superobjective [15]is dependent on
the actor's perspective of the Role [13] and the Through-
line of Action [14]. Next come the fundamentals of the performance, Physical Action [2] and the Given Circumstances or Pushkin's
Aphorism [3].

To operate within the principles of the System the actor has
three basic natural faculties, each subject to conscious control
in varying degrees – the Intellect [6], which can conceptualise
and make judgements and is available as a conscious instrument;
the Will [5], which is less subject to command; and Feeling [4],
which is least subject to command.

Experience [7], Physical Characterisation [8] and Reading [9] are
the strategies available during the preparation and rehearsal of
the play. [9] provides information about the Given Circumstances,
as set out in *Creating a Role*. On the left-hand side, are the
elements subsumed under experience, by and large set out in
An Actor Prepares, leading to the Internal Theatrical State [10].
On the right-hand side are the elements of Physical Characterisation, as set out in *Building a Character*, leading to the External
Theatrical State [11]. [10] and [11] combine to form the Common
Theatrical State [12].

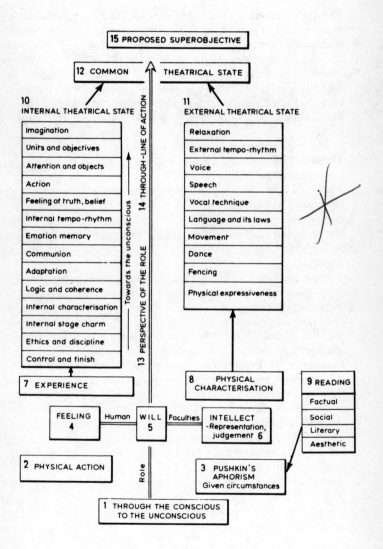

15 PROPOSED SUPEROBJECTIVE

12 COMMON   THEATRICAL STATE

10
INTERNAL THEATRICAL STATE

Imagination
Units and objectives
Attention and objects
Action
Feeling of truth, belief
Internal tempo-rhythm
Emotion memory
Communion
Adaptation
Logic and coherence
Internal characterisation
Internal stage charm
Ethics and discipline
Control and finish

11
EXTERNAL THEATRICAL STATE

Relaxation
External tempo-rhythm
Voice
Speech
Vocal technique
Language and its laws
Movement
Dance
Fencing
Physical expressiveness

14 THROUGH-LINE OF ACTION

— Towards the unconscious —

13 PERSPECTIVE OF THE ROLE

7 EXPERIENCE

8 PHYSICAL CHARACTERISATION

9 READING

Factual
Social
Literary
Aesthetic

FEELING 4	Human	WILL 5	Faculties	INTELLECT -Representation, judgement 6

2 PHYSICAL ACTION

Role

3 PUSHKIN'S APHORISM
Given circumstances

1 THROUGH THE CONSCIOUS TO THE UNCONSCIOUS

4

The Method of Physical Action

Dissatisfaction

In the last five years of his life Stanislavski's practice underwent almost as radical a change as it had undergone in the five years following his holiday in Finland. This time there was no immediate crisis to precipitate the change. On the contrary MXAT was highly successful, with an international reputation. Current methods were, by and large, producing results. None the less, Stanislavski was dissatisfied. It seemed to him that the integrity of the System needed to be re-established. He had spent many years analysing the creative process, breaking it down into its components. Now there was a need to re-emphasise its organic unity. Too often, in his view, actors and directors selected those parts of the System which appealed to them, or which they found the most easily accessible, and ignored the rest.

There were still, despite the overall success, basic difficulties, the most important of which remained the actors initial approach to a role. Stanislavski's insistence on the importance of the primary stage in the creation of a performance never varied and if there is a radical change in his ordering of the rehearsal process it arises from his perception that the synthesis of the elements of the System comes, not at the end, but is inherent at the very beginning, in the very first approach to the script.

The rehearsal methods Stanislavski had developed, were not being generally followed, or at least, they were not being adequately used. In the opening section of Part Three of *An Actor's Work on A Role*[1], Stanislavski writes in disillusioned terms, reminiscent of those in which he described the theatre practice current in his younger days.

The first acquaintance with a role, the approach to it, takes place, in the majority of theatres, in the following manner. The cast gathers to hear the play read to them. If the reading

[1] Cut in *Creating a Role*

is done by the author or someone who knows the work, so well and good. He need not be a good reader but he knows the inner line of the piece. Such people give a correct impression of the work and illuminate it. Unfortunately, quite often, the play is read by someone who does not know it. In these circumstances a somewhat distorted view is conveyed to the future interpreters of the text. This is extremely damaging since first impressions are deeply engraved on the actor's mind. It is difficult to correct these initial misunderstandings for the future creators of the new production.

After the first reading, in the majority of cases, the listeners have an impression of the work which is far from clear. To remedy that, a so-called 'chat' is organised. That is to say, the cast gathers together again and each member gives his opinion about the play he has heard. Views are rarely unanimous on any given point. More often than not they are quite contradictory and for the most disparate and unexpected reasons. Confusion reigns in the minds of those about to interpret the script.

Even those who apparently have some concept of work lose their grip on it. It is bad to be deprived of your opinions. After these chats the artists are as puzzled about their new roles as they would be if faced with a riddle they had to solve quickly. It is both painful and comic to see how defenceless they are. It is also deplorable and shameful because of the impotence of our psycho-technique. In order to penetrate the mysterious innermost depths of a part, artists not equipped with a system try to force an entry any way they can. Their only hope is that some happy accident will let them through. They can do no more than latch on to words like 'intuition', 'subconscious' which they do not, in fact, understand. If they are lucky and fortune is with them they regard it as an act of Providence, a gift from the gods.

If luck is not with them, they spend hours staring at an open script, trying all ways to get into the part, not only mentally but physically. Tense, exhausted by their efforts, they try to concentrate by mumbling the words of the text, which are quite foreign to them. Their gestures and facial expressions, which are not motivated from within, are not real, they are horrible grimaces. When no other help is forthcoming they get into costume and make-up so as to approach the part from the outside.

It is difficult to get into a body which is not one's own size. Where is the chink in the armour? The result is tension. Even those rare, vital moments which gave inner life and stirred the soul after the first reading come to an abrupt end and the artist stands before his role as before a stuffed dummy... What harm this does to his creative energy!

Unfortunately, in general, the cure was almost as bad as the disease. In criticising the remedy, Stanislavski was criticising practices he had himself instituted and which he now wished to revise.

To get them [the actors] out of trouble the director gathers all concerned round the table and spends several months analysing the play and the individual roles in detail. They talk about the play once more, saying whatever comes into their head. They exchange views, discuss with each other, invite specialists for various talks, read documents, hear lectures. They also look at sketches or models of the sets and costumes intended for the production. Then they decide, down to the most trivial detail what each of the actors will do, what each of them must feel, when, eventually, they get up on the stage and start to live their parts.

In the end the actor's heart and mind are filled with a mass of details, some useful, some not, like a chicken that has been fattened up by being stuffed with nuts. Not being in a position to absorb everything which has been violently crammed into his heart and mind the actor loses contact also with those rare moments when he was able to identify with the role.

And then they tell him, 'Get up on stage, play your part and apply everything you have learned in the recent months of group study.' With a stuffed head and empty heart the actor goes out on stage and simply can't do anything. More months are needed to get rid of all that is superfluous, to select and assimilate the essential, for him to discover himself – bit by bit, let us hope – in the part.

The question then arises whether it is right to force a part in the early stages when it is important to keep it fresh? Is it any good imposing ideas, judgements, perceptions about the part when the mind of the creative artist has not yet been opened up?

Of course, some things of value result from such work, enter his mind and help the creative process. But far more which is superfluous goes in too, unnecessary information, ideas and feelings which, initially, only clutter up the head and the heart, frighten an actor and inhibit his own free creation. To assimilate what is external and alien is more difficult than to create with one's own intelligence and heart.

But, worst of all, all these commentaries, coming from outside, fall on unprepared, untilled, arid soil. It is not possible to judge a work or the experiences it contains, if you have not recognised some part of yourself in the author's writing.

If the actor is in a prepared state to learn alien ideas and feelings armed with his internal forces and his external apparatus, which makes physical characterisation possible; if he feels firm ground beneath his feet, he will learn what he needs to accept or reject among the advice, useful or otherwise, which he is offered.[1]

Stanislavski confronted once more the problem of the actor divided against himself. But whereas in Red Square it was the actor as human being which was separated from the actor as performer, now the System, which had been designed to overcome that division, was, in its turn, dividing mind from body, knowledge from feeling, analysis from action. What Stanislavski had to seek was a *praxis*, theory and practice in organic unity.

Limitations of Emotion Memory

In reading a play an actor is called on to fill it out with his own memories and experiences, to give it human depth by his own personal involvement, through Emotion Memory. All too often, however, the evocation of past experiences produced negative results – tension, exhaustion, sometimes hysteria. At other times the mind seized up, refusing to yield up its secrets. Stanislavski had always been aware how carefully the evocation of emotion had to be handled. The unconscious cannot be commanded. Feelings have to be 'lured', 'enticed'. Now it seemed to him that any kind of direct attempt to evoke feeling or the memory of feeling had to be avoided. Just as it was wrong for an actor to be assaulted by a battery of outside fact and knowledge, so it was wrong for him to assault his own emotions.

[1] SS Vol. 4, pp. 313–5.

If the intellect can inhibit, and the emotions are fickle where can an actor begin in his exploration of a role? The answer is, with what is most immediately available to him, with what responds most easily to his wishes — his body.

The logic of physical action

Starting from the body Stanislavski developed a new method of approaching a role and new priorities for the initial stages of rehearsal.

There is a physical aspect to thought and a mental aspect to action.[1] Physical work can act as a powerful stimulus to the imagination and the unconscious. Stanislavski was aware of this and had used improvisation as early as 1905, but only as an adjunct and a support. In the classic model of MXAT rehearsals, physical action came last.[2] It was the bait with which to 'lure' the required feelings. During rehearsals for *The Battle of Life*, a Dickens adaptation, produced in 1924, he outlined his approach:

> First, everything has to be prepared so that the emotion will come; the actor's concentration and his correct state of being on stage at that particular moment, either in rehearsal or in performance... Second, you must define the exact feeling for each [unit]... Third, after having defined what feeling the actor must have, we must analyze the nature of this feeling... Fourth, after defining the nature of the feeling, the actor must search for actions which will arouse the feeling. This is the bait which the feeling will rise to. Fifth, having caught the feeling, he must learn to control it. Remember that it is the actor who controls the feeling, not the feeling which controls the actor.[3]

Just over a decade later, when Stanislavski was working on his final production, *Tartuffe*, it was a different story:

> At that time he considered the foundation of his System to be the work on physical actions, and he brushed away all that might distract the actors from its significance. When we reminded him of his earlier methods, he naively pretended that he didn't understand what we were talking about. Once someone

[1] AAP p. 144.
[2] CAR Part One.
[3] SD pp. 96–7.

asked: 'What is the nature of the "emotional states" of the actors in this scene?'

Constantin Sergeyevich looked surprised and said:

' "Emotional states" What is that? I never heard of it.'[1]

Later on in the same rehearsal he said:

Do not speak to me about feeling. We cannot set feeling; we can only set physical action.[2]

And again

Start bravely, not to reason but to act. As soon as you begin to act you will immediately become aware of the necessity of justifying your actions.[3]

The transition from one position to its opposite is charted in *An Actor's Work on a Role* (*Creating a Role*). In Part One (1916–20), which describes work on Griboyedov's *Woe from Wit*, the stage of physicalisation comes last, after exhaustive textual and psychological analysis. In Part Two (1930–33), work on *Othello* begins with a reading by Stanislavski/Tortsov. Physical work follows immediately after, now preceding any detailed textual study. In Part Three (1936–7) the students are plunged immediately into a physical exploration of *The Government Inspector*.

In the method of Physical Action, or, more accurately, the Method of Analysis through Physical Action, the actor starts by creating, *in his own person*, very often in precise detail, a logical sequence of actions, based on the question, 'What would I do *if…*', the 'if' being his intentions within the given circumstances of the play. At this stage he is using his own words, not the author's. The actor's total being is therefore engaged from the start. The circumstances and the actions they prompt become, in the process of exploration, a personal reality.

In real, everyday life people behave in a logical, coherent manner in their internal and external actions, either consciously or from force of habit. In the majority of cases we are driven by our life goals, absolute need, human necessity. People usually react instinctively, without thinking. But on stage, playing a role,

[1] SIR p. 157.
[2] SIR p. 160.
[3] SIR p. 161.

life is created not by authentic necessity but by the products of our imagination. On stage, before creative work begins, there are no human necessities, vital living needs, in the actor's mind, which correspond to the goals of the character. These necessities, these goals, cannot be created all at once but develop gradually, during the long period of creative work.[1]

The logic and coherence of physical actions, directed to a given end (What do I want and what do I do to get it?) results in a logical, coherent psychological life.

An actor on the stage need only sense the smallest modicum of organic physical truth in his action or general state and instantly his emotions will respond to his inner faith in the genuineness of what his body is doing. In our case it is incomparably easier to call forth real truth and faith within the region of our physical than of our spiritual nature. An actor need only believe in himself and his soul will open up to receive all the inner objectives and emotions of his role...[2]

Inseparable from the notion of action is the question of rhythm. Body rhythms are a powerful trigger for the emotions. Thus Stanislavski's earlier insistence on the importance of tempo-rhythm acquires even greater importance:

You cannot master the method of physical actions if you do not master rhythm. Each physical action is inseparably linked with the rhythm which characterises it.[3]

Emotion as action

Complex and difficult emotions are also broken down into a series of actions. How, Stanislavski asks, can you act 'love'? Certainly not by attempting to evoke the feeling direct. The solution is to imagine a series of happenings, or moments, which add up to the emotion. The emotion becomes a story in which each moment is represented by a single action. In other words, true to earlier discoveries, emotion becomes a process and not a question

[1] SS Vol. 2, pp. 380–1.
[2] CAR p. 150. See also p. 239.
[3] SIR p. 170.

of imitation. If the sequence of actions is sufficiently well worked out the actor can take off, like an aeroplane.[1]

The analytic process, however, whether physical or intellectual, needs to be counterbalanced by a sense of the whole. Experience had shown that too great a preoccupation with individual units and objectives led actors to forget the overall meaning of the play. There were many objectives but no superobjective. The through-line of action was blurred. Stanislavski now proposed that the play should be broken down into longer sequences, which he called 'events'. A work might only contain three or four major events, each of which would necessitate a number of actions all tending towards the same goal. The event, for example might be, 'entering a drama school'.[2] This would require the applicant to accomplish a number of actions over a fairly lengthy period. They would however only have significance in relation to each other. The actor, in consequence, instead of getting bogged down in the minutiae of his role, is obliged to think forward, *i.e.* dynamically, projecting forward the whole time.

The text

Having established firm contact with the material of the play in his own person the actor is then ready to start taking on the specific characteristics of the role, almost by osmosis. There is to be no forcing, no attempt to cram his nature into an alien mould. He is also ready for the author's text now that the necessity for it has been created and it can be seen as the inevitable expression of all that has gone before. Analysis and study then become vital and creative functions.

By holding back the text until a later stage of rehearsals Stanislavski was by no means devaluing it, or suggesting it was of secondary importance to physical, or non-verbal expression. On the contrary he regarded verbal action as the most artistically satisfying and expressive of all. He was greatly concerned to keep the text fresh. Words mechanically repeated during rehearsals without meaning or justification became merely lodged in the muscles of the tongue and no more.

[1] SL pp. 46–7.
[2] Maria Knebel in *K. Voprosou o Metodye Deistvennovo Analiza*, in *Voprosi Teatralnovo Iskousstva*, Moscow, 1978, pp. 110–111.

Treasure the words of a text for two important reasons: first, not to wear the sheen off them, and second not to introduce a lot of mechanical patter, learned by rote and bereft of soul, into the sub-text of the play.[1]

The system restructured

In developing a new working method, Stanislavski did not in any way contradict anything he had written or taught about the 'grammar' of acting. The Method of Physical Action can only really be practised by those who have mastered the psycho-physical technique outlined in both parts of *An Actor's Work on Himself*. What the new method does is to bring all the elements of the System into greater unity by making them organic to the actor and his process.

In 1938 Stanislavski planned a production of *Tartuffe* which was to demonstrate his new method. The choice of a classic play in verse, rather than a more obviously 'naturalistic' piece, was deliberate and designed to prove the universal applicability of the System. He died while the play was still in rehearsal although he had done enough work for the performance to go forward. He thus left no formal description of the new method nor was he able to complete the task of revising and reshaping his sequence of books in the light of his new discoveries. Only some drafts and notes remain.[2] It has fallen to his young colleagues and collaborators of the time, some of them still teaching in Moscow, to explain and develop his last experiments.[3]

[1] CAR p. 141.
[2] See Appendix.
[3] For an account of the *Tartuffe* rehearsals, see SIR.

5

The Progress of an Idea

Stanislavski's ideas did not win immediate acceptance, not even among his closest colleagues. The radical revision of his approach to the problems of acting and directing which he announced on his return from Finland in 1906 and again his change of method in 1933 were resisted. Even Nemirovich was not fully convinced, despite the public support he gave, even, on one occasion, dressing down the entire company whom he considered were being obstructive.

It was principally to young actors that Stanislavski turned and whom, with the support of a few faithful friends, he trained. He realised early on that rehearsals are not the best place to teach the System.[1] As a result four Studios for actors were founded between 1912 and 1921 to teach students, together with an opera studio in 1924 for singers. In the thirties it was with a group of friends and young actors that Stanislavski worked on the Method of Physical Action. This is not to say that Stanislavski himself was not respected as an artist, even venerated, but this respect did not entail automatic acceptance of his theories. The working methods of MXAT were often subject to derision and ridicule even as late as 1930. It is only perhaps in the post-war period that, in the Soviet Union, the Stanislavski System has become the cornerstone of training.

Outside Russia Stanislavski's ideas have been frequently mis-understood. There are historical reasons for this. Originally they were brought to the west by actors who had worked either at MXAT or in one of the Studios and had experience of the System in action. The question is _when_ they were taught and at what stage of the System's development. Grotowski has expressed the problem concisely

> During the numerous years of research [Stanislavski's] method evolved, but not his disciples. Stanislavski had disciples for each of his periods and each disciple is limited to his particular

[1] SD pp. 192-3.

period; from that came discussions like those of theology. He himself was always experimenting and did not suggest recipes but the means whereby the actor might discover himself, replying in all concrete situations to the question: 'How can this be done?'[1]

A case in point is Richard Boleslavsky, who had taken part in the crucial production of *A Month in the Country* in 1908 and had left the company to emigrate to the United States in 1922. His exposition of the System is clear and coherent but he was necessarily unaware of the last phase of Stanislavski's activity.[2] His influence on acting in America was profound.

In 1923 Boleslavsky founded the American Laboratory Theatre and was joined by Maria Ouspenskaya who stayed in the United States after the end of the MXAT tour.[3] Among their pupils was Lee Strasberg. Boleslavsky's teaching was heavily dependent on the notion of Emotion Memory, which, under the influence of Strasberg, became the cornerstone of the Method, itself the subject of much discussion and debate in Britain in the nineteen-fifties.

The Method has become popularly identified with the System, although Strasberg himself was well aware of the differences. When Stella Adler, who had been working with Stanislavski in Paris, outlined the new Method of Physical Action to him in 1934 he rejected it. For him the fundamental element in acting was the recollection of emotion.[4] The result can be an introverted form of acting. The Method tends to replace the given circumstances by the actor's biography, the character's psychology by the actor's personality. The actor does not restructure elements of himself to reveal the meaning of the text so much as draw the text within the ambit of his own experience. In the hands of star players it can produce charismatic results. Used by lesser talents the results can often be self-indulgent and stultifying.[5]

[1] Jerzy Grotowski, *Towards a Poor Theatre*, London, Methuen, 1969, p. 206.
[2] Boleslavsky, *Acting: The First Six Lessons*, New York, Theatre Arts Books, 1949. See also Cole and Chinoy (eds.), *Actors on Acting*, New York, Crown, 1970.
[3] *Actors on Acting*, p. 510.
[4] *The Stanislavski Heritage*: Letter from Lee Strasberg to Christine Edwards, p. 261.
[5] *There is a Method in British Acting* quoted in *The Stanislavski Heritage*, pp. 268–9.

It was precisely these lesser talents, however, that the System was designed to help.

A further hindrance to proper understanding is the erratic way in which Stanislavski's books have appeared. This is due largely to editorial problems and the accident of war. *My Life in Art* was first published in the United States in 1924. *An Actor Prepares* appeared in the United States in 1936 but the complementary volume, *Building a Character* was not issued until fourteen years later, in 1950. There was a further gap of eleven years before the publication of *Creating A Role* in 1961. Under these circumstances the coherence and wholeness of Stanislavski's scheme is hard to grasp.

Stanislavski is identified principally with two books, the unrevised version of *My Life in Art*[1] and *An Actor Prepares*, which is actually half a book.

Now, more than forty years after Stanislavski's death and with a considerable body of published work, including drafts for revised chapters and notes,[1] it is possible to take an over-view and see the System as a whole.

The Stanislavski System is not important as a set of exercises or precepts, which if religiously followed will result in good acting. Knowledge of grammar is no guarantee of being able to write imaginatively; an ability to manipulate the figures of rhetoric will not create poetry. Grammar provides a structure within which the creative mind can operate. The System is important because it draws attention to certain precise questions and suggests methods for solving them. The solutions cannot simply be repeated, or imitated – that is the return to the cliché. The questions arise each time a play goes into rehearsal. What Stanislavski offers is a process of decision-making that does not do violence to the actor and his creative possibilities.

> The 'System' is a guide. Open it and read it. The 'System' is a reference book, not a philosophy. Where philosophy begins the 'System' ends. You cannot act the 'System': you can work with it at home but on stage you must put it on one side.
>
> There is no 'System'. There is only nature. My life's object has been to get as near as I can to the so-called 'System', i.e. to the nature of creation.
>
> The laws of art are the laws of nature. The birth of a child,

[1] See Appendix.

the growth of a tree, the creation of a character are manifestations of the same order. The establishment of a 'System', i.e. the laws of the creative process, is essential because on the stage, by the fact of being public, the work of nature is violated and its laws infringed. The 'System' re-establishes these laws; it advances human nature as the norm. Turmoil, fear of the crowd, bad taste, false traditions deform nature.

The first aspect of the method is to get the unconscious to work. The second is, once it starts, to leave it alone.[1]

[1] SS Vol. 3, p. 309. See also BAC Chap. XVI.

Appendix

There are significant differences between the Soviet edition of Stanislavski's works and the available English translations. The Russian edition of the Complete Works, published between 1951 and 1964, was established by an editorial committee which included members who had worked closely with Stanislavski himself and is based on a collation of all the available manuscripts and variants in the MXAT Museum Archives. It consists of the following volumes:

1. *My Life in Art.*
2. *An Actor's Work on Himself in the Creative Process of Experience.*
3. *An Actor's Work on Himself in the Creative Process of Physical Characterisation.*
4. *An Actor's Work on a Role.*
5. *Essays, Articles, Speeches,* etc. 1877–1917.
6. *Essays, Articles, Speeches,* etc. 1917–38.
7. *Letters,* 1886–1917.
8. *Letters,* 1917–38.

Volumes 5–8 have not been translated into English. This edition is shortly to be replaced by a 12-volume edition.

The following notes indicate the areas in which English-language editions differ from the Soviet edition.

My Life in art was commissioned by an American publisher to coincide with the MXAT's U.S. tour. It was dictated to O.F. Boshkansakaya during 1922 and 1923 and translated chapter by chapter. The book was, by Stanislavski's own admission, hastily put together. Stanislavski's memory for facts and dates was not good. He even got the timing of his historic meeting with Nemirovich wrong, stating that it began at ten in the morning, whereas, in fact, it began at two in the afternoon. He decided that the book should be revised for the first Russian edition and asked Mrs Gurevich to help him. The American edition translated by J. J. Robbins appeared in 1924, the Russian in 1926.

The text was revised again in 1936, when Stanislavski saw

it as part of his planned sequence of works. The version which forms Volume 1 of the Complete Works is fuller than the one available in English. In particular the final chapters are longer and more informative, especially where the growth of the System is concerned.

There is also a change of chapter order which makes Stanislavski's development much clearer. Although discussions with Gordon Craig concerning *Hamlet* began in 1908, the first night did not occur until January 1912. In order to understand the evolution of Stanislavski's thinking, it is better therefore to adopt the Russian order and read chapter 57 after chapter 53 so that the relationship of the production of the production of *A Month in the Country* to the conclusions reached in Finland is more apparent.

The Soviet edition also publishes, in an Appendix, passages which Stanislavski cut on the advice of friends.

An Actor Prepares also first appeared in the United States. In 1928 Stanislavski suffered a heart attack. He went to Baden-weiler to be treated by Chekov's doctor. There he joined Norman and Elizabeth Hapgood with whom he had formed a close friendship in New York in 1923 during the American tour. They added their voices to the many others who were urging him to put his teaching into permanent form. The Stanislavski family moved to Nice where they stayed for several months with the Hapgoods as their neighbours. Stanislavski continued work on *An Actor Prepares* which was in draft form. Mrs Hapgood translated the manuscript into English, while Norman Hapgood, who was an experienced editor and drama critic, was active with a red pencil suggesting cuts and changes. Mrs Hapgood translated her husband's suggestions back into Russian for Stanislavski's approval. Stanislavski signed a contract with Mrs Hapgood giving her full power of attorney to act on his behalf in receiving royalties for him and his heirs and in negotiating contracts. As Stanislavski wrote to Mrs Gurevich in December 1930, the shape of the book at the end of 1930 was largely due to Norman Hapgood's advice. That same year a contract was signed with Yale University Press. A completed Russian text was forwarded to the Hapgoods in New York in 1935 and Mrs Hapgood devoted the next two years to preparing the final English translation. On receiving the manuscript YUP rejected it as uncommercial mainly because of repetitions. In 1935 Theatre Arts Books accepted the book on the condition that further cuts were made. Stanislavski agreed. The work was published in 1936. In 1936, apparently to establish US copyright, Mrs Hapgood registered herself and her husband as co-authors. The joint copyright of this, and of Stanislavski's other published works, was renewed in 1964. After the first Russian edition appeared in 1938 Mrs Hapgood's excisions were severely criticised. To counter mounting hostility Theatre Arts Books engaged an expert to make a detailed comparison of the original and the translation. This resulted in a notarised statement declaring that, apart from the deletion of repetitions, the two texts were identical. Later criticism[1] has, however, called the accuracy of the translation and the wisdom of the cuts into doubt. The 1954 Soviet edition, Volume 2 of the Complete Works, is based on further scholarship. Stanislavski continued work on the book after the American edition and even after he had delivered the manuscript to the Russian publishers in 1937. The Soviet edition therefore contains new drafts, passages for insertion, corrections etc., which are published as a supplement. This includes:

1. For the chapter on Action.
2. For the chapter on Communion.
3. On the interaction of actor and audience.
4. On the actor's invention.

These show how Stanislavski would have modified the text to give his total scheme more coherence and to bring it more into line with the Method of Physical Action.

Building A Character is far more problematic. There are wider differences between the English and Russian editions. In 1937 Mrs Hapgood visited Moscow and Stanislavski promised her the manuscript. His death in 1938 and the war the following year delayed delivery until the late forties. Publication was planned for 1948 but was delayed until 1949, as Mrs Hapgood had received new material sent by Stanislavski's son, Igor, in accordance with his father's wishes.

The Soviet version, which forms Volume 3 of the Complete Works, appeared in 1955. It is substantially based, as stated in Chapter Three, on the editorial work affected, partly under Stanislavski's supervision, by G. Kristi. The Notes contain details of the

[1] Carnicke, Sharon M., *An Actor Prepares* in Theatre Journal, December 1984, pp. 481–494.

archive material which has been selected and the way in which it has been put together. As with preceding volumes supplementary material is provided – revisions, new passages for insertion – in preparation for a reworking of the whole. There are also draft teaching programmes for both actors and singers.

A comparison of the contents page of *Building a Character* and the chapter sequence of *An Actors Work on Himself, Part Two*, reveals major differences. Each book contains material absent from the other. Where chapters cover the same topic, different variants, of which there could be many, have been used. Thus while conceptually the books are close, at the level of the text they are widely disparate.

We are therefore faced with two versions of the same work, based on two separate sets of editorial decisions. The Soviet edition of 1955, in common with other volumes produced as part of the Complete Works in the oppressive Stalinist atmosphere of the 1950's, was doctored for ideological reasons in order to bring Stanislavski's texts into line with the official doctrine of Socialist Realism. The cuts will be restored in the new Soviet nine-volume edition.

Creating A Role, published in the U.S.A. in 1961 and in the Soviet Union, as Volume 4 of the Complete Works in 1957 do correspond, apart from some cuts. As before the Soviet edition contains additions and revisions in the Appendices.

Stanislavski's Legacy, first published in the U.S.A. in 1958, is a collection of articles and fragments, which contain some of the material to be found in additional material published in the Appendices of the Complete Works, or among the Essays. These are not, in general, related to Stanislavski's overall plan.

Index of Topics

The following is a list of the major topics referred to in the text